The Lighthouse Companion for Connecticut and Rhode Island

Photographs by Paul Rezendes

Published by Tide-mark Press
Windsor, Connecticut

Published by Tide-mark Press Ltd.
P.O. Box 20, Windsor, CT 06095-0020

Printed in Korea by Samhwa Printing Co.

Design by Paul G. Rasid

Copyright 2003 by Paul Rezendes and Tide-mark Press

All rights reserved.
No part of this book may be reproduced in any form
or by any electronic or mechanical means
without written permission from the publisher;
reviewers, however,
may quote brief passages in the context of a review.

First Edition

ISBN 1-55949-741-6

Table of Contents

Introduction to Connecticut Lighthouses 4
Avery Point Lighthouse 6
Faulkners Island Light 8
Fayerweather Island Light 10
Five Mile Point Lighthouse 12
Great Captain Island Lighthouse 14
Greens Ledge Light 16
Lynde Point Light 18
Morgan Point Lighthouse 20
Mystic Seaport Lighthouse 22
New London Harbor Lighthouse 24
New London Ledge Lighthouse 26
Peck Ledge Light 28
Penfield Reef Light 30
Saybrook Breakwater Lighthouse 32
Sheffield Island Light 34
Southwest Ledge Light 36
Stamford Harbor Light 38
Stonington Harbor Lighthouse 40
Stratford Point Lighthouse 42
Stratford Shoal Light 44
Tongue Point Light 46

Introduction to Rhode Island Lighthouses 48
Beavertail Lighthouse 50
Bristol Ferry Light 52
Castle Hill Lighthouse 54
Conanicut North Light 56
Conimicut Point Light 58
Dutch Island Lighthouse 60
Gooseberry Island Light 62
Hog Island Shoal Light 64
Nayatt Point Lighthouse 66
Newport Harbor Light 68
North Light 70
Plum Beach Light 72
Point Judith Lighthouse 74
Pomham Rocks Lighthouse 76
Poplar Point Light 78
Rose Island Lighthouse 80
Sakonnet Point Lighthouse 82
Sandy Point Lighthouse 84
Southeast Light 86
Warwick Light 88
Watch Hill Lighthouse 90
Appendix 92
Bibiliography 105
Index 106

Connecticut Lighthouses

Stonington Harbor Lighthouse

Connecticut has enjoyed a long maritime history, due to its location on Long Island Sound and the presence of the Connecticut River. Native Americans, the state's first residents, used the state's waterways for transportation and sustenance. Commercial vessels used in the trading industry sailed here as early as the seventeenth century and were later replaced with a steamboat service that ran from New York City to Hartford. By the eighteenth and nineteenth centuries, shipbuilding had become one of the state's largest industries.

Lighthouses first began to appear on the Connecticut coast in 1823, when the Stonington Harbor Lighthouse was erected on Windmill Point. Since then, there have been twenty-three beacons built on the shoreline of the "Charter Oak State," twenty-one of which are still active. As you will see in the following pages, the stories of Connecticut's lighthouses are imbued with history, a sense of romance, and even the occasional ghost story!

Connecticut Lighthouse Locations by Number

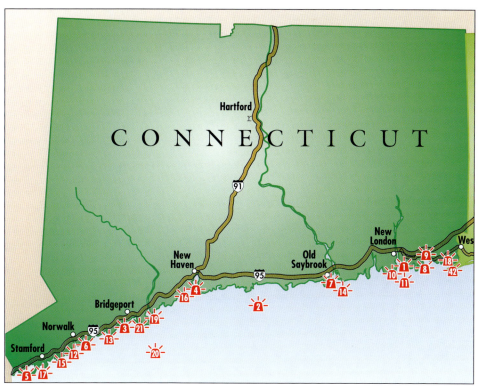

Lighthouse Number	Lighthouse Name	Page
1	Avery Point Lighthouse	6
2	Faulkners Island Light	8
3	Fayerweather Island Light	10
4	Five Mile Point Lighthouse	12
5	Great Captain Island Lighthouse	14
6	Greens Ledge Light	16
7	Lynde Point Light	18
8	Morgan Point Lighthouse	20
9	Mystic Seaport Lighthouse	22
10	New London Harbor Lighthouse	24
11	New London Ledge Lighthouse	26
12	Peck Ledge Light	28
13	Penfield Reef Light	30
14	Saybrook Breakwater Lighthouse	32
15	Sheffield Island Light	34
16	Southwest Ledge Light	36
17	Stamford Harbor Light	38
18	Stonington Harbor Lighthouse	40
19	Stratford Point Lighthouse	42
20	Stratford Shoal Light	44
21	Tongue Point Light	46

Avery Point Lighthouse

Latitude: 41° 18' 55" N
Longitude: 72° 03' 49" W

The University of Connecticut grounds in Groton, Connecticut.

Avery Point Lighthouse

Groton, Connecticut

Directions:
Take I-95 to exit 87 (CT 349, Clarence B. Sharp Highway) in Groton. Turn right at the second traffic light onto Rainville Avenue. Turn left at the next light onto Benham Road. Continue straight for approximately 1.7 miles to the Avery Point Campus of the University of Connecticut. Take the second entrance onto the campus. Continue straight to the waterfront. Parking is available in front of the Project Oceanology building. The lighthouse can also be viewed on DownEast Lighthouse Cruises, based in Groton. Call (860) 445-9729.

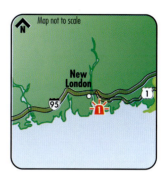

The last lighthouse built in Connecticut, Avery Point Lighthouse was built on United States Coast Guard grounds as a ceremonial light tower that serves as a symbol of the group's work with lighthouses and the sea. Avery Point Lighthouse was first lighted on May 2, 1944 and initially exhibited a fixed white light, which was changed to a flashing green beacon on March 3, 1960.

The 55-foot tower was operated privately until the Coast Guard left the area on June 25, 1967, at which point the light was extinguished. Shortly thereafter, the University of Connecticut established a campus on the property and in 1997, officials from the Avery Point campus, which now surrounds the lighthouse, called for a restoration of the deteriorating tower. The Avery Point Lighthouse Society was formed in 2000 to raise funds for the effort. In December 2001, the first major renovation began on the tower's lantern room. Fund-raising efforts for the restoration of the tower continue today.

Contact Information:
Avery Point Lighthouse Society
P.O. Box 1552
Groton, Connecticut 06340
(860) 445-5417
Website: http://apls.tripod.com

Faulkners Island Light

Contact Information:
Faulkners Light Brigade
P.O. Box 199
Guilford, Connecticut 06437
(203) 453-8400

Latitude: 41° 12' 42" N
Longitude: 72° 39' 12" W

Faulkners Island Light

Guilford, Connecticut

Directions:
The lighthouse can be seen distantly from Guilford. From I-95 North or South: Take exit 58 and follow CT 77 (Church St.) into Guilford Center. Turn right on Broad Street, then left on Whitfield, and follow to a marina with free parking. The lighthouse can be seen to the south.

Originally called Falcon Island by the English because of the many falcons that once resided here, Faulkners Island lies approximately three miles south of Guilford Harbor. The water here is shallow and dangerous reefs abound. In 1802, President Thomas Jefferson commissioned a lighthouse and wooden keeper's house to be built on the island and Faulkners Island Light became the second lighthouse in Connecticut. Built by stonemason Abisha Woodward (who also built New London Harbor Lighthouse), the brick-lined tower stands 46 feet.

One of Faulkners Island's most famous keepers was Captain Oliver Brooks, who served from 1851 to 1882. Throughout his 31 years of service, Captain Brooks attended to approximately 100 ships. After rescuing five passengers from the wrecked schooner *Moses F. Webb* in November 1858, he was awarded a gold medal by the New York Life Saving Society.

The keeper's house was replaced in 1871 with an eight-room, three-story structure. Unfortunately, the house burned down in 1976, and the fire caused extensive damage to the tower as well. The light was repaired and automated in 1978, and new windows and doors were installed.

Unfortunately, the lighthouse's problems continue. Because of erosion, the light now stands approximately 35 feet from the edge of the island. Thanks to the nonprofit organization Faulkners Light Brigade, the lighthouse was completely restored in late 1999, and erosion control measures have been implemented by the Army Corps of Engineers.

Fayerweather Island Light

Latitude: 41° 08' 32" N
Longitude: 73° 13' 02" W

Contact Information:
Fayerweather Island
Restoration Fund
c/o Burroughs Community Center
2470 Fairfield Avenue
Bridgeport, Connecticut 06605
(203) 334-0293

Fayerweather Island Light

Also known as Black Rock Harbor Light
Bridgeport, Connecticut

Directions:
From I-95 North or South: Take exit 26, bear right onto Admiral Street. Turn right on Iranistan Avenue and right again at Sound View Drive onto P.T. Barnum Boulevard. Follow to the park. There is a charge to enter the park, but if you explain that you plan a short stay to see the lighthouse, you might be allowed in without paying. Follow Barnum Boulevard to a parking area near a fishing pier and the sand spit leading onto Fayerweather Island. It's about a 20-minute walk to the lighthouse.

In 1807, the government purchased nine and one-half acres of land from David Fayerweather with the purpose of building a lighthouse to mark the entrance of Black Rock Harbor. The 40-foot octagonal tower was completed the following year but was destroyed in a hurricane in 1821.

Architects of the second lighthouse, which was completed the following year, were determined to build a tower that would withstand rough weather conditions. An 1850 inspection found that the tower was as sturdy as the builders claimed. A new lantern was installed and a fifth-order Fresnel lens replaced the old lanterns.

After its decommissioning in 1933, the lighthouse was given to the city of Bridgeport and became part of the town's Seaside Park. Unfortunately, the next few decades saw the neglected tower fall into ruin and fall victim to vandals.

Two local residents established a preservation and restoration fund for Fayerweather Island Light in 1993. Thanks to their efforts, the tower has been repainted and relit. According to the Fayerweather Island Restoration Fund that continues to work to improve the lighthouse, public tours and historical plaques may be in the tower's future.

Five Mile Point Lighthouse

Latitude: 41° 14' 57" N
Longitude: 72° 54' 13" W

Contact Information:
Lighthouse Point Park
Lighthouse Road
New Haven, Connecticut 06515
(203) 946-8005
Website: www.newhavenparks.org/lighthouse_point.htm

Five Mile Point Lighthouse

Also known as New Haven Harbor Light
New Haven, Connecticut

Directions:
From I-95 North or South: Take exit 50N or 51S to Townsend Avenue. Follow signs for Lighthouse Point Park to Lighthouse Road and turn right into the entrance to the park.

One of New England's most prosperous cities, New Haven was a hub of coastal and West Indies trade in the early nineteenth century. The first lighthouse was built here in 1805 and was nicknamed Five Mile Point Lighthouse, to represent the distance it stood from downtown New Haven. The 30-foot light was considered too short and too dim from its inception. To add to its problems, trees in the area began to obstruct views of the lighthouse's signal.

The current beacon was built here in 1840 to replace the obsolete 1805 structure. It stands 70 feet tall and is built of sandstone from East Haven and lined with brick from New Haven. The attached keeper's dwelling is painted red. The lighthouse's twelve lamps and reflectors were replaced with a fourth-order Fresnel lens in 1855, and a fog bell was added a few years later.

Five Mile Point Lighthouse was discontinued in 1877 when the Southwest Ledge Light was activated. Today it is owned by the city of New Haven and stands near the city's only public swimming beach in Lighthouse Point Park.

Great Captain Island Lighthouse

**Contact Information:
Greenwich Town Hall
101 Field Point Road
Greenwich, Connecticut 06830
(203) 622-7814**

Latitude: 40° 58' 54" N
Longitude: 73° 37' 24" W

Great Captain Island Lighthouse

Greenwich, Connecticut

Directions:
The lighthouse cannot be seen from the mainland. There is a ferry to the island for Greenwich residents only. Call (203) 622-7818 for information on the ferry. The lighthouse may be visible from some of the cruises aboard the schooner *SoundWaters* out of Stamford; call (203) 323-1978 for information.

Great Captain Island lies approximately 1 mile off the coast of the town of Greenwich. Open only to Greenwich residents, the 17-acre property is home to a picnic area, beaches, and a lagoon. Local legend states that the island is also thought to be home to Captain Kidd's buried treasure.

The original lighthouse and five-room keeper's cottage were built in 1829 on the southeast end of the island. Inspections over the next few decades proved that the lighthouse was poorly constructed as walls were cracked and windows often leaked. Although a new fourth-order Fresnel lens installed in 1858 improved the dim lighting in the lighthouse, the decision was made to replace the building.

A stone lighthouse was built on the same spot in 1868. It was fitted with the previous structure's fourth-order Fresnel and received a fog whistle in 1890. In 1907, a steam whistle replaced the original fog signal. A compressed air siren was later installed. Great Captain Island Lighthouse was automated in 1970, but a caretaker still resides in the keeper's house to prevent vandalism.

In 1998, the Greenwich Chamber of Commerce started a campaign to relight Great Captain Island Lighthouse.

Greens Ledge Light

Latitude: 41° 02' 30" N
Longitude: 73° 26' 36" W

Greens Ledge Light

Norwalk, Connecticut

Directions:
From I-95 North: Take exit 12 to CT 136. Follow CT 136 for about 0.5 miles, then turn right on Roton Avenue. Bear left onto connecting Pine Point Road, then turn right on Pine Point Terrace. Turn left at Gull Road, then right at Ensign Road. Turn left at Crescent Beach Road and continue onto South Beach Drive. The lighthouse can be seen offshore as you drive along the beach. It can also be seen distantly from the ferry from Norwalk to Sheffield Island; call the Norwalk Seaport Association at (203) 838-9444 for more information.

This "sparkplug-shaped" light was commissioned by the government in 1896 to mark the entrance to Norwalk Harbor. Completed in 1902 at a cost of approximately $60,000, Greens Ledge Light was originally fitted with a fifth-order Fresnel lens that exhibited a flashing red light. The lantern soon was upgraded to a fourth-order lens that exhibited a white light interspersed with red flashes.

Greens Ledge Light was automated in 1972 and fitted with a modern rotating lens. The light and accompanying fog signal continue to serve as active navigation aids under the auspices of the United States Coast Guard.

Lynde Point Light

Latitude: 41° 16' 18" N
Longitude: 72° 20' 36" W

First lit on August 17, 1803, Lynde Point Light was built to mark the entrance to the Connecticut River. The wooden tower stood 35 feet tall and was octagonal in shape. By 1838, however, the original tower was replaced with the current 65-foot, brownstone structure.

Lynde Point Light

Also known as Saybrook Lighthouse
Old Saybrook, Connecticut

Directions:
The lighthouse station is not accessible to the public. It can be seen from various points in the area. From I-95 North: Take exit 67 to Elm Street and turn right. Cross US 1 to CT 154 (Main Street), follow CT 154 to the left to Saybrook Point. From I-95 South: Take exit 69 to US 1. Continue into Old Saybrook Center on US 1/CT 154; bear left and follow CT 154 (Main Street) to Saybrook Point. From Saybrook Point, continue 0.5 miles to the South Cove Bridge and causeway. The lighthouse can be seen from this area. As you continue on CT 154, the lighthouse can be seen from several vantage points, including Knollwood Beach (1.9 miles from Saybrook Point). This and other area lighthouses can also be seen from lighthouse cruises offered by Captain John's Sport Fishing Center in Waterford, (860-443-7259) and DownEast Lighthouse Cruises in Groton (860-445-9729). Deep River Navigation Company in Deep River, Connecticut, offers cruises on the Connecticut River from Saybrook Point; call (860) 526-4954. In addition, Camelot Cruises in Haddam, Connecticut, offers cruises on the Connecticut River and Long Island Sound; call (860) 345-8591.

Although similar masonry was used in the construction of nearby New London Ledge Lighthouse and Faulkners Island Light, Lynde Point is thought to be the finest building of the three.

A seawall was constructed around the tower in 1829 to combat erosion from strong river currents and was widened and reinforced three years later. In 1852, the lighthouse's system of ten lamps and reflectors was replaced by a fourth-order Fresnel lens. Thirty-eight years later, the lamp was downgraded to a fifth-order lens. Lynde Point Light was electrified in 1955 and automated in 1978.

The old keeper's house was demolished in 1966 and replaced with a modern duplex to house Coast Guard employees.

Morgan Point Lighthouse

Contact Information:
Noank Historical Society Museum
17 Sylvan Street
Noank, Connecticut 06340
(860) 536-7026

Latitude: 41° 19' 00" N
Longitude: 71° 59' 23" W

Morgan Point Lighthouse

Noank, Connecticut

Directions:
This lighthouse is privately owned and not open to the public. It is best seen from the water. Mystic Seaport, a large museum complex in Mystic, offers a ride aboard the vintage steamer *Sabino* that travels down the Mystic River as far as Morgan Point. Call (860) 572-5351 for details. Captain John's Sport Fishing Center in Waterford, Connecticut, offers an excellent lighthouse cruise that includes Morgan Point Light; call (860) 443-7259 for information. DownEast Lighthouse Cruises in Groton also offers views of Morgan Point Lighthouse. Call Captain Jeff at the Pine Island Marina at (860) 445-9729.

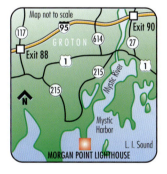

The Morgan Point Lighthouse stands at the mouth of the Mystic River on land purchased from an ancestor of James Morgan, who originally settled the area. A 25-foot circular granite tower and separate keeper's house were built here in 1831, but as the town's fishing and shipbuilding industries multiplied in the 1860s, the need for a new lighthouse became apparent.

The second lighthouse at Morgan Point began operation in 1868. Among the updated aspects of the light were a combined tower and keeper's house. The new tower was equipped with the sixth-order Frensel lens that had replaced the ten lamps and reflectors in the prior tower in 1855. The lighthouse was discontinued in 1919 when an automatic electric light was placed at the channel entrance to the Mystic River. Morgan Point Lighthouse is now privately owned, but the Noank Historical Society has a collection of historical items from the site.

Mystic Seaport Lighthouse (Brant Point Light Replica)

Latitude: N/A
Longitude: N/A

Contact Information:
Mystic Seaport
P.O. Box 6000
75 Greenmanville Avenue
Mystic, Connecticut 06355-0990
(860) 572-0711
Website: http://www.mysticseaport.org

Mystic Seaport Lighthouse

Also known as Brant Point Light (Replica)
Mystic, Connecticut

Directions:
From I-95 South: Take exit 90 and turn left at the end of the ramp onto Route 27 South. Proceed approximately one mile. Pass North Parking lot on left (opposite Seamen's Inne). Mystic Seaport South Parking is the second lot on your left and opposite the main entrance to the Visitor Center. This lot provides the easiest access point to the Museum. From I-95 North: Take exit 90. From the right lane, turn right at the light onto Route 27 South. Proceed approximately one mile. Pass North Parking lot on left (opposite Seamen's Inne). Mystic Seaport South Parking is the second lot on your left and opposite the main entrance to the Visitor Center. This lot provides the easiest access point to the Museum.

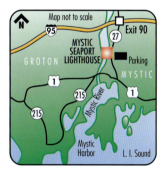

Mystic Seaport is a replica of an authentic nineteenth-century coastal village featuring tall ships, fisheries, and exhibits on such historic activities as ropemaking, barrelmaking, and boatbuilding. In the heart of the village is a reproduction of Nantucket's (Massachusetts) original Brant Point Light, built in 1746. A plaque on the lighthouse in Mystic Seaport details the construction and history of the 250-year-old beacon.

The original Brant Point Light, America's third oldest light station, was appropriated by Nantucket merchants and mariners at a town meeting in January 1746. The prosperous whaling town necessitated a beacon to help ships navigate into the town's inner harbor. Two hundred English pounds were raised to fund the lighthouse, which was constructed of wood over the next few years. Unfortunately, the lighthouse was burned to the ground in a 1757 fire.

New London Harbor Lighthouse

Latitude: 41° 19' 00" N
Longitude: 72° 05' 24" W

As New London's whaling industry began to thrive in the eighteenth century, the need became apparent for a lighthouse to mark the entrance to the Thames River. The 64-foot granite tower constructed here in 1760 became

New London Harbor Lighthouse

New London, Connecticut

Directions:
From I-95 North: Take exit 82A to Colman Street and turn right (exit 82B if southbound). Turn left at Bank Street, then right at Shaw Street onto connecting Pequot Avenue. The lighthouse is just south of Montauk Avenue on Pequot Avenue. You can see the lighthouse from the sidewalk; do not enter the station as it is private property. The lighthouse can be clearly seen from the Fishers Island, Block Island, Montauk Point, and Orient Point ferries leaving New London. It can also be viewed from the excellent lighthouse cruises offered by Captain John's Sport Fishing Center in Waterford (860-443-7259), and by DownEast Lighthouse Cruises in Groton. Call Captain Jeff at (860) 445-9729.

the fourth lighthouse built in the United States. Funds for the lighthouse's construction and upkeep were raised through a lottery and through a tonnage tax imposed on shipping. During the Revolutionary War, light from the tower's lantern helped American privateers find shelter from British warships.

By 1799, a ten-foot fracture had developed in the tower and mariners complained that the light was ineffective. A new 89-foot, octagonal-shaped lighthouse was completed in 1801. Unlike the Revolutionary War, where the beacon played a significant role, New London Harbor Lighthouse was extinguished by Americans during the War of 1812 so the British could not navigate the harbor.

New London Harbor Lighthouse can be seen from Pequot Avenue in New London. Several local boat tours and ferries also pass the lighthouse, including those going to Fishers Island and Block Island.

New London Ledge Lighthouse

Latitude: 41° 18' 18" N
Longitude: 72° 04' 42" W

Contact Information:
New London Ledge Lighthouse Foundation
P.O. Box 855
New London, Connecticut 06320
(860) 442-2222

New London Ledge Lighthouse

New London, Connecticut

Directions:
Tours are run by Project Oceanology on the University of Connecticut's Avery Point Campus in Groton. To get there, leave I-95 at exit 87 (CT 349, Clarence B. Sharp Highway). Turn right at the second traffic light onto Rainville Avenue. Turn left at the next light onto Benham Road. Continue straight for approximately 1.7 miles to the Avery Point Campus. Take the second entrance onto the campus. Continue straight to the waterfront. Parking is available in front of the Project Oceanology building. DownEast Lighthouse Cruises in Groton also offers views of the lighthouse. Call (860) 445-9729.

The three-story New London Ledge Lighthouse is easily recognizable by its bright red bricks, white trim, and French Second Empire-style architecture, all of which are elements incorporated to be in keeping with the elegant architecture of the coastal New London community. One of the last lighthouses built in New England, construction began on the lighthouse in 1906 after mariners complained of a need for a signal to warn of the 200-foot shoal where the lighthouse sits. The Hamilton R. Douglas Company of New London completed work on the lighthouse in 1909, and it was fitted with a rotating fourth-order Fresnel lens. New London Ledge Lighthouse was automated in 1987 and today is powered by solar panels and an underwater cable.

Local legend recounts the tale of a former keeper who is said to have jumped to his death after discovering his wife ran off with a ferry captain. "Ernie" is said to haunt the building today, setting off the fog horn, opening and closing doors, and untying secured boats in the area.

New London Ledge Lighthouse can be viewed from the shore of New London and also from the Fishers Island and Block Island ferries that depart from New London.

Peck Ledge Light

Latitude: 41° 04' 36" N
Longitude: 73° 22' 12" W

Peck Ledge Light

Norwalk, Connecticut

Directions:
This lighthouse can be viewed from Calf Pasture Park in South Norwalk. From I-95 North: Take exit 16 to East Avenue, take a left onto CT 136 (Cemetery Street), then follow as the road merges onto Gregory Boulevard. Follow Gregory Boulevard south through a curve to the left (around a monument) to the Fifth Street and Calf Pasture Beach Road intersection. Turn right onto Calf Pasture Beach Road and continue to Calf Pasture Park. Towards your left at the entrance is a large parking area from which the lighthouse can be seen. The view is fairly distant; bring your binoculars. The park is open year-round, sunrise to sunset. There is a parking fee during the summer. The lighthouse can also be seen distantly from the ferry to Sheffield Island, which departs from the Hope Dock near the Maritime Aquarium in Norwalk. Call (203) 838-9444 for more information.

Peck Ledge Light is situated on the east end of the Norwalk Islands. Although a light was proposed here years earlier, Peck Ledge Light was not completed until 1906, four years after the station at nearby Greens Ledge was built. The light was designed with a cylindrical, cast-iron foundation and took the form of other sparkplug lights in the area. Inside the lighthouse are three floors of living space, topped by a lantern fitted with a fourth-order Fresnel lens.

The lighthouse was staffed for only twenty-seven years before becoming automated in 1933. Although the original lens was replaced, the lighthouse continues to exhibit a flashing white light to guide mariners.

Penfield Reef Light

Latitude: 41° 07' 00" N
Longitude: 73° 13' 18" W

Penfield Reef Light

Fairfield, Connecticut

Directions:
The lighthouse can be seen fairly distantly from Fairfield Beach. From I-95, take exit 22 to Round Hill Road and turn right. Follow Round Hill Road across US 1 (Boston Post Road) onto Beach Road. Turn right at Fairfield Beach Road. Follow the road south through a zig-zag intersection. A short distance from the intersection on the left is a narrow lane, across the street from College Place. Parking is not allowed on Fairfield Beach Road near the lane. Park on Reef Road or another side street. The lane to the beach is marked with "Lighthouse Point" and "Penfield Reef Right of Way" signs. Walk down the lane to the beach. The lighthouse can be seen about 1.3 miles off to the southwest.

Penfield Reef Light, established on January 16, 1874, was designed by famed nineteenth-century lighthouse architect F. Hopkinson Smith, who also designed Rhode Island's Race Rock Light. The construction plan for the light consisted of a two-story stone house meant to serve as keeper's quarters built onto a cylindrical stone pier. A 35-foot octagonal tower sits atop the keeper's quarters and originally held a fourth-order Fresnel lens exhibiting a flashing red light every six seconds.

Legend states that the ghost of keeper Frederick Jordan haunts the area. Jordan, who drowned while in transit to the mainland for Christmas leave in 1916, has been known to tinker with the light and save mariners in distress in stormy weather conditions.

In 1969, the Coast Guard announced plans to demolish the current tower, but the plan was never carried out, thanks to a significant outpouring of support from local residents. Automated in 1971, Penfield Reef Light continues to serve as a navigational aid today, thanks to a modern DCB-24 aerobeacon and an automated electric horn that emits a blast every fifteen seconds.

Saybrook Breakwater Lighthouse

Latitude: 41° 15' 48" N
Longitude: 72° 20' 36" W

Saybrook Breakwater Lighthouse

Old Saybrook, Connecticut

Directions:
Saybrook Breakwater Lighthouse can be seen from points on CT 154 in Old Saybrook, but is best viewed from the water. This and other area lighthouses can be seen from lighthouse cruises offered by Captain John's Sport Fishing Center in Waterford. Call (860) 443-7259 for details. Deep River Navigation Company in Deep River, Connecticut, offers cruises on the Connecticut River from Saybrook Point, call (860) 526-4954. Camelot Cruises in Haddam, Connecticut, also offers cruises on the Connecticut River and Long Island Sound, call (860) 345-8591. You can also call DownEast Lighthouse Cruises in Groton at (860) 445-9729.

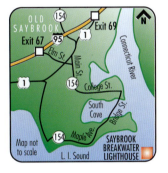

In 1886, the Saybrook Breakwater Lighthouse, commonly known as the "Outer Light," was built 1.5 miles across from the Lynde Point Light to assist in marking the entrance of the mouth of the Connecticut River. The 49-foot cast-iron tower stands on a concrete foundation and consists of a basement, four main floors, a watch deck, and a lantern room.

Since 1889, the lighthouse held a 1,000-pound fog bell, but after complaints from local residents, the bell was replaced with a 250-pound model. This was eventually replaced with two fog horns that continue to sound every thirty seconds. Likewise, the seventeen lamps and fixed red and white fifth-order Fresnel that originally fitted the lighthouse were replaced with a new fourth-order lens in 1890.

Automated in 1959, a new modern optic at Saybrook Breakwater Lighthouse continues to flash green every six seconds.

Sheffield Island Light

Latitude: 41° 02' 56" N
Longitude: 73° 25' 09" W

**Contact Information:
Norwalk Seaport Association
132 Water Street
South Norwalk, Connecticut 06854
(203) 838-9444
Website: www.seaport.org**

Sheffield Island Light

Norwalk, Connecticut

Directions:
To visit Sheffield Island, you must board a ferry from the Hope Dock. From I-95 North: Take exit 14N and follow Fairfield Avenue and Reed Street to West Avenue. Turn right onto West Avenue. At the West Avenue–M. L. King–North Main Street intersection, bear left onto North Main Street. Turn left at Ann Street, then continue to North Water Street and a municipal parking lot where all-day parking is available for a fee. Parking tickets can be validated at the Maritime Aquarium. The Hope Dock is right next to the Aquarium. From I-95 South: Take exit 15S and bear right at the fork. At the bottom of the ramp, turn left at West Avenue. From there the directions are the same as from I-95 North.

The first lighthouse built on this island off the coast of Norwalk was operational as early as 1826. It had a small, stone keeper's house and an unusual lighting system that consisted of ten lamps and reflectors, powered by a rotating clockwork mechanism that flashed alternating red and white lights. In 1857, the system was replaced with a fourth-order Fresnel lens.

This lighthouse was replaced in 1868 with a stone Victorian-style building. Although deactivated in 1902 after the construction of Greens Ledge Light to the west, Sheffield Island Light is still open to the public. The Norwalk Seaport Association owns this historic building, which is powered by a generator. Sheffield Island Light can be reached by ferry from Norwalk.

Southwest Ledge Light

Latitude: 41° 14' 06" N
Longitude: 72° 54' 42" W

Southwest Ledge Light

Also known as New Haven Breakwater Light
New Haven, Connecticut

Directions:
Southwest Ledge Light can be seen distantly from Lighthouse Point Park in New Haven. From I-95 North or South: Take exit 50N or 51S to Townsend Avenue. Follow to Lighthouse Road and turn right into the entrance to the park. The lighthouse can also be seen from some of the sightseeing cruises on the *Liberty Belle* out of New Haven. Call (203) 562-4163 for more information.

Southwest Ledge Light is built on a dangerous rock formation that sits approximately 1 mile from New Haven Harbor. While it was recommended that a light be built here in 1845, the government's budget did not allow construction until 1877. The lighthouse represented the latest in technology both in its cylindrical iron structure and powerful octagonal lantern. In fact, a model of the superstructure was displayed at the 1876 Centennial Exposition in Philadelphia, where an actual lighthouse keeper maintained a light in the tower throughout the show. This model later became Ship John Shoal Light, stationed in Delaware. Due to its optimum performance, Southwest Ledge Light put nearby Five Mile Point Lighthouse out of commission upon its activation.

A fourth-order Fresnel lens was installed in the new beacon and a fog signal followed a few years later. Poor conditions at the lighthouse, including leaky walls, undrinkable water, and an infestation of cockroaches, led to a high turnover rate in keepers over the years. Finally, the light was automated in 1973. With the help of a modern lens installed in 1988, the lighthouse continues to serve mariners today.

The lighthouse can be seen at a distance from New Haven's Lighthouse Park and from sightseeing tours that depart from the area.

Stamford Harbor Light

Latitude: 41° 00' 54" N
Longitude: 73° 32' 18" W

Stamford Harbor Light

**Also known as Chatham Rocks Light
Stamford, Connecticut**

Directions: The lighthouse can be seen from the Shippan Point section of Stamford. From I-95: Take exit 8 to Elm Street. Turn right at Jefferson Street, then left at Magee Street, and straight through an intersection where it becomes Shippan Street. Turn right at Ocean Drive, then right at Fairview Avenue. Park on the side of Fairview Avenue and walk down to the small beach at its dead end. The lighthouse can be seen near the West Breakwater. It may also be possible to see the lighthouse from some of the cruises on *SoundWaters*, a schooner based in Stamford. Call (203) 323-1978 for details.

Although stationed off the shore of Connecticut, Stamford Harbor Light was built in Boston, Massachusetts. After construction of the various sections of the 60-foot cast-iron tower was complete, each was transported to Chatham Rocks and assembled on the site where the finished tower still stands.

The lighthouse, fitted with a fourth-order Fresnel lens and equipped with a fog bell, went into service in 1882. It remained in service for more than eighty years, but was eventually deactivated in 1953. The lighthouse has had a series of private owners over the last five decades and is currently for sale for the asking price of $1.1 million.

Stonington Harbor Lighthouse

Latitude: 41° 19' 43" N
Longitude: 71° 54' 20" W

Contact Information:
Stonington Historical Society
P.O. Box 103
Stonington, Connecticut 06378
(860) 535-1440
Website: www.stoningtonhistory.org/light.htm

Stonington Harbor Lighthouse

Stonington, Connecticut

Directions:
Take exit 91 off I-95 and turn south on Route 234 (Pequot Trail). Continue nearly 0.5 miles to North Main Street. Turn left and stay on North Main for 1.5 miles to the light at the intersection with Route 1. Cross Route 1 and continue straight to a stop sign. Turn left onto Trumbull Avenue and then take a right onto Alpha Avenue, over the railroad bridge, to Water Street. Follow Water Street through historic Stonington Village to the end. Park at the Point and walk up to the lighthouse. The lighthouse can also be viewed on DownEast Lighthouse Cruises offered by Captain Jeff at Pine Island Marina in Groton. Call (860) 445-9729.

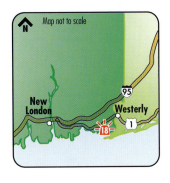

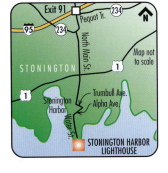

The Stonington Harbor Lighthouse was activated in 1824 to help whaling and fishing ships navigate Fishers Island Sound and Stonington Harbor. The first tower built at the end of the mile-long peninsula known as Stonington Borough consisted of a small keeper's house and a 30-foot granite tower. Upon inspection in 1838, it was discovered that erosion had moved the lighthouse nearly 25 feet. In addition, the silver coating on the reflectors had been worn thin from polishing and the tower's wooden stairway was deteriorating quickly. Rather than spending the time and money to repair the lighthouse, the federal government made the decision to replace the building.

The current 35-foot granite tower and keeper's house were built in 1840. In 1856, a sixth-order Fresnel lens replaced the former system of eight lamps and a series of reflectors. Although the light was discontinued upon construction of the Stonington Breakwater Light in 1889, the Stonington Harbor Lighthouse was purchased by the Stonington Historical Society in 1925 and serves as a historical museum today.

Stratford Point Lighthouse

Latitude: 41° 09' 06" N
Longitude: 73° 06' 12" W

Stratford Point Lighthouse

Stratford, Connecticut

Directions: The keeper's house is used as housing for a Coast Guard family and there is no public access. The lighthouse is best viewed from the water.

The Stratford Point Lighthouse was built in 1822 to warn mariners of the shifting sand bars, rugged cliffs, and strong currents that exist at the mouth of the Housatonic River. Before the light was built, a bonfire and then an iron basket on a pole were used as navigational aids at this location.

In 1881, a cone-shaped, cast-iron, brick-lined tower replaced the original octagonal wooden structure. The 35-foot tower is painted white with a red band in the middle and originally held a third-order Fresnel. In 1969, the original lantern was removed from Stratford Point Lighthouse to make way for the most powerful lighting system of any Connecticut lighthouse at the time, a system of DCB-224 rotating lights. The lantern was placed on display at Stratford's Boothe Memorial Park. Twenty years later, however, the lantern was reinstalled and the aerobeacons were replaced with a 190-millimeter modern optic, which is the lighting system that stands intact today.

The keeper's dwelling, rebuilt in 1881, now houses a Coast Guard family.

Stratford Shoal Light

Latitude: 41° 03' 36" N
Longitude: 73° 06' 06" W

Stratford Shoal Light

Also known as Middleground Light
Bridgeport, Connecticut

Directions: Stratford Shoal Light is best seen by private boat, but it can be seen distantly from the Bridgeport-Port Jefferson (New York) Ferry. Call (203) 367-3043 for information. The ferry carries passengers and autos year-round and there are frequent departures from both ports.

Although many navigational aids, including fixed-spar buoys and a lightship, were used at Stratford Shoal in earlier centuries, the Lighthouse Board called for the establishment of a permanent fixture in 1872. One of the last granite island lighthouses built, Stratford Shoal Light became operational in December 1877. The lighthouse tower, originally equipped with a fourth-order Fresnel, stands 35 feet high and its flashing white light has a focal plane height of 60 feet. In 1879, a fog bell was added to the building. The bell was replaced several times over the years and the light presently houses an automatic fog signal that emits one blast every fifteen seconds. Likewise, Stratford Shoal Light's Fresnel lens was replaced several times over the years— by fourth-order Fresnels in 1894 and 1905, by a 300-millimeter optic in 1988, and, most recently, by the 190-millimeter, solar-powered lens that continues to power the light today.

Stratford Shoal Light has been automated since 1970.

Tongue Point Light

Latitude: 41° 10' 00" N
Longitude: 73° 10' 42" W

Tongue Point Light

Also known as Bridgeport Breakwater Light
Bridgeport, Connecticut

Directions:
Tongue Point Light is on the grounds of a large power station; the grounds are not open to the public. A close view of this lighthouse is available from the Bridgeport-Port Jefferson (New York) Ferry. Call (203) 367-3043 for information. The ferry carries passengers and autos year-round and there are frequent departures from both ports.

Tongue Point Light, notable because of its black paint scheme, marks an 11,000-foot breakwater built in Bridgeport Harbor. The 31-foot, cast-iron lighthouse, built in 1895, was installed with a sixth-order Fresnel lens exhibiting a fixed white light. A fog bell was added eight years later. No keeper's quarters were built at Tongue Point Light—rather, the duties of looking after the structure were given to the keeper of Bridgeport Harbor Light. Not surprisingly, the double burden left the keeper ragged and a 1901 inspection found that Bridgeport Harbor Light was in poor condition. As a result, Bridgeport Harbor Light's keeper, Stephen McNeil, was given the sole duty of looking after Tongue Point Light. McNeil built a small shack near the lighthouse, where he stayed to carry out his duties for the length of his position.

In 1920, the shipping channel at Bridgeport Harbor was widened, necessitating a shorter breakwater. Because of this, Tongue Point Light was relocated 275 feet inland. The lighthouse was automated in 1954 and continues to serve as an active aid to navigation, exhibiting a green flash from its modern 155-millimeter optic every four seconds.

Tongue Point Light sits on land that is currently owned by a utility company. It is not accessible to the public and can be seen only by boat.

Rhode Island Lighthouses

Conimicut Point Light

Although it may be small in size, Rhode Island has a surprisingly large number of lighthouses on its coastline. The "Ocean State" is home to twenty-one beacons, thirteen of which are active. In addition, visitors can view several former light stations where tower foundations are still visible. Included in this collection is the site of Lime Rock Light, which has since been converted to the Ida Lewis Yacht Club in Newport. Although a decorative light displayed seasonally is all that remains of this historic light station, the site has an intriguing history.

Idawalley Zoradia Lewis was a sixteen-year-old girl when her parents' health prevented them from their lightkeeping duties at Lime Rock Light. A strong swimmer, Ida assumed these duties with energy. Throughout her fifty-five years as keeper of Lime Rock Light, Ida is thought to have rescued as many as twenty-five mariners and became the most celebrated lighthouse keeper in American history. She made the covers of *Harper's Weekly* and *Frank Leslie's Illustrated Newspaper*, was the subject of the "Ida Lewis Waltz," and received a visit from United States President Ulysses S. Grant, who said, "I have come to see Ida Lewis, and I'd get wet up to my armpits if necessary."

While not listed in this publication, Lime Rock Light is a site that Rhode Island lighthouse lovers will not want to miss. The yacht club is not open to the public, but views are available of this and most other Rhode Island lighthouses from the many harbor cruises that are offered in the area.

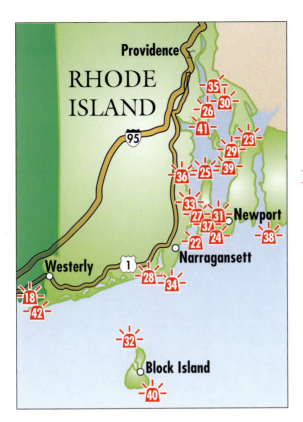

Rhode Island Lighthouse Locations by Number

Lighthouse Number	Lighthouse Name	Page
22	Beavertail Lighthouse	50
23	Bristol Ferry Light	52
24	Castle Hill Lighthouse	54
25	Conanicut North Light	56
26	Conimicut Point Light	58
27	Dutch Island Lighthouse	60
28	Gooseberry Island Light	62
29	Hog Island Shoal Light	64
30	Nayatt Point Lighthouse	66
31	Newport Harbor Light	68
32	North Light	70
33	Plum Beach Light	72
34	Point Judith Lighthouse	74
35	Pomham Rocks Lighthouse	76
36	Poplar Point Light	78
37	Rose Island Lighthouse	80
38	Sakonnet Point Lighthouse	82
39	Sandy Point Lighthouse	84
40	Southeast Light	86
41	Warwick Light	88
42	Watch Hill Lighthouse	90

Beavertail Lighthouse

Latitude: 41° 26' 58" N
Longitude: 71° 23' 59" W

**Contact Information:
Beavertail Lighthouse
Museum Association
P.O. Box 83
Jamestown, RI 02835
Website:
www.beavertaillight.org**

Beavertail Lighthouse is the third oldest lighthouse in America. Established in 1749 at the tip of Conanicut Island, the lighthouse replaced the bonfire and fog cannon that had served to mark the entrance to Narragansett Bay since 1705. The original 58-foot wooden tower burned down within a few years and was replaced in 1753 by a 64-foot stone beacon, fitted with a system of 15 lamps and reflectors. Tariffs on harbor use funded the upkeep of the tower in its early years, although expenses quickly surpassed the amount of income generated.

Beavertail Lighthouse

Jamestown, Rhode Island

Directions:
Beavertail Lighthouse may be reached via Route 138 from the east or west side of Narragansett Bay. After crossing the Jamestown Bridge (from North Kingstown) or the Newport Bridge (from Newport), follow the signs to Jamestown Center. Continue southward past Mackerel Cove Town Beach to Beavertail State Park at the tip of the island, where there is free parking. A view is also possible from the lighthouse cruises offered periodically by Bay Queen Cruises in Warren, Rhode Island. The cruise provides good views of a number of Narragansett Bay and Mount Hope Bay lighthouses. Call Bay Queen cruises at (401) 245-1350 or visit www.bayqueen.com for details. You can also see the lighthouse from trips offered aboard the sailing vessel *Mai Ling*; call (401) 965-5154 for details or visit the *Mai Ling* website at www.mai-ling.com.

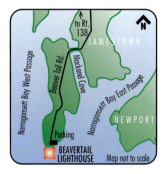

Beavertail Lighthouse has a fascinating history. In 1817, the structure became the first lighthouse to be lit by gas, during an experiment by Newport inventor David Melville. Although gas proved to burn cleaner and brighter, opposition by the whale oil industry caused the government not to pursue usage of the new energy source. The British burned the lighthouse upon retreating from Newport Harbor in 1779, but President George Washington called for the lighthouse to be repaired and reactivated in 1790.

The current 45-foot granite structure was built in 1856 and was fitted with a third-order Fresnel lens. One year later, the nation's first steam-powered foghorn was added. Automated in 1972, Beavertail Lighthouse remains an active aid to navigation for the United States Coast Guard. The assistant keeper's house, built in 1898, has been converted into a historical museum and houses the beacon's fourth-order Fresnel, which was installed in 1975, but replaced by a modern rotating beacon in 1991.

Bristol Ferry Light

Latitude: 41° 38' 35" N
Longitude: 71° 15' 37" W

Bristol Ferry Light

Bristol, Rhode Island

Directions:
From RI 114 North or South: Travel until you reach the Mount Hope Bridge (toll) exit in Bristol. Turn east onto Ferry Road. Continue to a large turnaround. Parking is not permitted in the turnaround, so park on Ferry Road. You can view the lighthouse from the nearby rocky beach, but please remember to respect the privacy of the residents. You can also view Bristol Ferry Light from the lighthouse cruises offered periodically by Bay Queen Cruises in Warren, Rhode Island. The cruise provides good views of a number of Narragansett Bay and Mount Hope Bay lighthouses. Call Bay Queen cruises at (401) 245-1350 for details.

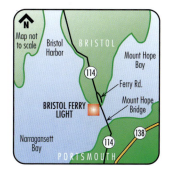

Although a private beacon had been maintained in the Narragansett Bay by the Fall River Steamboat Company since 1846, a petition to the Lighthouse Board by local ship captains prompted the construction of the Bristol Ferry Light at the entrance to Bristol Harbor in 1855. The 28-foot, white-brick, square tower, attached to a keeper's house, was positioned in the narrow passage between Mount Hope Bay and Narragansett Bay and was fitted with a sixth-order Fresnel that displayed a fixed white light visible for up to 11 miles at sea. It was first lit on October 4, 1855.

The light was upgraded to a fifth-order lens in 1902 and in 1916, the wooden lantern room was replaced by an iron version that was taken from a deactivated lighthouse. The tower was also raised 6 feet during its time of service.

In 1927 the lighthouse was decommissioned and replaced by a steel skeleton tower, which in turn was replaced by the Mount Hope Bridge in 1929. Since 1929, Bristol Ferry Light has been privately owned. It can be viewed from the north side of the Mount Hope Bridge, along with the original 1855 keeper's house and 1904 oil house.

Castle Hill Lighthouse

Latitude: 41° 27' 42" N
Longitude: 71° 21' 48" W

Castle Hill Lighthouse

Newport, Rhode Island

Directions:
In Newport, take America's Cup Avenue and Thames Street (one way) to Wellington Avenue and turn right. Turn left at Halidon Avenue, then right onto Harrison Avenue. Turn right onto Castle Hill Road, then left onto Ocean Drive. Turn right at a paved road with a small "Inn at Castle Hill" sign. Turn right to the Castle Hill Cove Marina and park there. The lighthouse is reached via a quarter-mile trail that begins opposite the marina entrance. It leads over a hill and to concrete steps leading to the lighthouse. You can also see the lighthouse from trips offered aboard the sailing vessel *Mai Ling*; call (401) 965-5154 for details or visit the *Mai Ling* website at www.mai-ling.com.

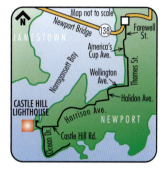

Congress first proposed the establishment of a lighthouse on Castle Hill in 1875, but construction was halted for several years due to the opposition of noted Harvard professor and naturalist Alexander Aggasiz, who argued that the beacon would encroach on his property. While waiting for the dispute to be resolved, steamboat companies painted the rocky cliffs of Castle Hill white to serve as a marker. In 1886, Aggasiz finally relented and sold his property on Castle Hill to the government.

The 34-foot granite structure was first lit on May 1, 1890 and was fitted with a fifth-order Fresnel lens and a fog bell. Its style has been described as "Richardsonian Romanesque," a term that refers to famed architect H.H. Richardson, who is thought to have helped design Castle Hill Lighthouse.

The upper half of the all-gray tower was painted white in 1899. Castle Hill Lighthouse was automated in 1957 and continues to exhibit a flashing red light across Narragansett Bay as an active aid to navigation today. The light is not open to the public, but the grounds are accessible and are just a short walk from the Castle Hill Inn.

Conanicut North Light

Latitude: 41° 34' 24" N
Longitude: 71° 22' 18" W

Conanicut North Light

Jamestown, Rhode Island

Directions: From RI 138 in Jamestown, take East Shore Road north. At the northern tip of the island, where East Shore turns west, turn right onto a dirt road. The lighthouse is about one tenth of a mile from the turn.

The square, wooden tower and six-room Gothic Revival-style keeper's quarters that serve as Conanicut North Light were built in 1886 to help mariners navigate the dangerous north point of Conanicut Island. The black lantern was originally fitted with a fifth-order Fresnel lens that displayed a fixed white light, but a new optic with a fixed red light was substituted in 1907.

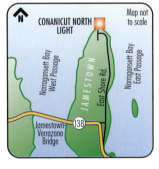

In 1933, Conanicut North Light was replaced by an automatic light on a steel skeleton tower, which was discontinued altogether in the 1980s. The original lighthouse was sold at auction and is now privately owned. The tower has since been painted red with white trim, and the lantern house has since been removed and capped. Along with the tower, the lighthouse's original 1897 barn and 1901 brick oil house still stand.

Conimicut Point Light

Latitude: 41° 43' 00" N
Longitude: 71° 20' 42" W

Conimicut Point Light

Warwick, Rhode Island

Directions:
Conimicut Point Light can be seen from Conimicut Point Park in Warwick. From I-95 North or South: Take exit 13 to the Airport Access Road. Follow the road onto RI 117 (West Shore Road). The road eventually becomes Bush Avenue. Turn left at Symonds Avenue, then right at Point Avenue and follow to the park. The park is open year-round, sunrise to sunset, but there is a parking fee from July to Labor Day. Conimicut Point Light can also be seen from the area around Nayatt Point in Barrington, and a good view is possible from the lighthouse cruises offered periodically by Bay Queen Cruises in Warren, Rhode Island. The cruise provides good views of a number of Narragansett Bay and Mount Hope Bay lighthouses. Call Bay Queen cruises at (401) 245-1350 for details.

The 58-foot lighthouse that marks Conimicut Point Shoal today is the second lighthouse to be built in this location. The first, a granite tower with no accompanying keeper's dwelling, was constructed in 1868. Until 1882, when an updated tower was built on the spot, keepers resided at the nearby discontinued Nayatt Point Lighthouse and rowed to Conimicut Point to tend to the lighthouse.

The new lighthouse built at Conimicut Point was designed in the sparkplug style of Connecticut's Stamford Harbor Light, with living quarters built into the structure. A fourth-order Fresnel lens exhibited a fixed white light and a red sector was added later. In 1960 Conimicut Point Light was the last American lighthouse to become electrified; three years later, the beacon became automated as well. Conimicut Point still serves as an active aid to navigation under the auspices of the United States Coast Guard.

Dutch Island Lighthouse

Latitude: 41° 29' 48" N
Longitude: 71° 24' 16" W

Contact Information:
Dutch Island Lighthouse Society
P.O. Box 40151
Providence,
Rhode Island 02940

Dutch Island became a major trading center in the 1630s as the West India Company bartered novelties in exchange for furs, meat, and fish from the Indians. As traffic increased in the area, the government allocated funds for a lighthouse to mark the west passage of Narragansett Bay that led to Dutch Island Harbor.

Dutch Island Lighthouse

Jamestown, Rhode Island

Directions:
Dutch Island Lighthouse can be viewed from the Fort Getty Recreation Area in Jamestown. Eastbound on RI 138: Cross over the Jamestown Bridge and continue to an exit just west of the Newport Bridge, marked with a "Jamestown" sign. Westbound on RI 138: Cross over the Newport Bridge to the Jamestown exit. Then follow Wolcott Avenue south; turn right at Hamilton Avenue, then left at Southwest Avenue to the entrance to the Fort Getty Recreation Area. There are day fees and camping fees in the park, though you may be allowed a free short stay if you state that your purpose is to visit the lighthouse. Follow the loop road around the park until it reaches the high ground by the bay with a view of Dutch Island.

The first lighthouse built here in 1826 was constructed of stones from the island. A 42-foot brick tower and keeper's house were built here in 1857 and the light was fitted with a fourth-order Fresnel lens. Gun batteries built during the Civil War years were expanded in the twentieth century and became a military camp known as Fort Greble. Men stationed at this fort in 1923 noticed a fire that had gotten out of hand at Dutch Island Lighthouse and stopped the blaze from destroying the beacon.

In 1924, the fixed white light was changed to a flashing red signal and automated in 1947. Frequent vandalism to the abandoned beacon prompted the Coast Guard to discontinue the light in the 1970s, and in 1979, Dutch Island Lighthouse was sold to the state of Rhode Island.

In 2000, the Dutch Island Lighthouse Society was formed to restore the historic beacon. The group is raising funds and accepting donations for a complete renovation of the Dutch Island Lighthouse, which has been recognized as a national historic landmark. The tower, though not open to the public, is currently part of the Bay Islands State Park.

Gooseberry Island Light

Latitude: 41° 23' 07" N
Longitude: 71° 31' 08" W

This privately owned stone, aluminum, and glass structure was built over a period of five years and completed in 1999. It stands 35 feet tall and is topped by a lantern room that overlooks Gooseberry Island's marshes and ponds and the Atlantic Ocean.

The lighthouse was the brainstorm of John Hooper, a retired football coach and inventor from New Jersey who has always been drawn to lighthouses. He began pursuing his dream of owning his own "toy" beacon over a decade ago, when he and his family bought a piece of property in Snug Harbor and filed for a permit.

Gooseberry Island Light

Wakefield, Rhode Island

Directions: This lighthouse is privately owned and not open to the public. It is best seen from the water. Southland Cruises in Galilee offers a ride aboard the *Southland Riverboat* that has an excellent view of the lighthouse. Call (401) 783-2954 for details. Gooseberry Island Light can also be seen from Snug Harbor Marina in Wakefield, Rhode Island.

After much research, Hooper began working on a model of the structure and an attached replica seventeenth-century cottage. Hooper and his family began collecting rocks from old construction sites and Hooper himself used an electric winch to position and mortar the stones.

Companies in Rhode Island, Maine, and Texas were hired to provide the different parts of the lighthouse, including the spiral staircase and aluminum frame to hold the windows above the stone walls. The lantern room, the most intricate part of the project, was constructed in Galilee, Rhode Island, by Jay and David Gallup of Rhode Island Engine. Hooper and his daughter-in-law, engineer Kimberly Hooper, worked with the Gallups using computer-assisted-design technology to create the final design. The Gallups then welded the industrial-strength diamond-plate aluminum to match the blueprints and delivered it in 1999.

Although United States Coast Guard regulations prevent the Hoopers from installing a beacon in the tower, the family plans to furnish the lighthouse with maritime antiques, including an authentic telescope, ship's wheel, and binnacle.

Hog Island Shoal Light

Latitude: 41° 37' 54" N
Longitude: 71° 16' 24" W

Hog Island Shoal Light

Portsmouth, Rhode Island

Directions:
From RI 114 South: You can see the lighthouse offshore to the right as you cross the Mount Hope Bridge. Just after crossing the bridge, turn right onto a cloverleaf interchange. Circle around to Bristol Ferry Road and turn left. Cross a set of railroad tracks. Drive straight ahead to the old ferry wharf. From RI 114 North: Drive straight ahead onto Bristol Ferry Road as you approach the Mount Hope Bridge. The view is fairly distant; bring your binoculars. A good view is also possible from the lighthouse cruises offered periodically by Bay Queen Cruises in Warren, Rhode Island. The cruise provides good views of a number of Narragansett Bay and Mount Hope Bay lighthouses. Call Bay Queen cruises at (401) 245-1350 for details.

A privately owned lighted ship marked this dangerous spot in the east passage of the Narragansett Bay for twenty years before it officially became established as a light station. In 1886, the 72-foot Hog Island Shoal Lightship was officially stationed at the south end of the island to mark the shoals surrounding Bristol Harbor.

The last lighthouse to be built in Rhode Island, Hog Island Shoal Light was built in 1901 to replace the lightship. The 60-foot, cast-iron structure was supported by a series of caissons and designed in the sparkplug style that was popular at the time. The black lantern atop the white tower was fitted with a fifth-order Fresnel lens, which was upgraded to a fourth-order Fresnel in 1903. Hog Island Shoal Light was automated in 1964, and its 250-millimeter optic continues to welcome mariners to the bay with a six-second intermittent flashing white light.

Nayatt Point Lighthouse

Latitude: 41° 43' 31" N
Longitude: 71° 20' 20" W

Nayatt Point Lighthouse

Barrington, Rhode Island

Directions: Nayatt Point Lighthouse can be seen from Barrington Town Beach. The beach is open only to residents of Barrington in the summer, but is open to everyone in the off-season. A good view is also possible from the lighthouse cruises offered periodically by Bay Queen Cruises in Warren, Rhode Island. Call Bay Queen cruises at (401) 245-1350 for details.

Nayatt Point Lighthouse was constructed in 1828 to assist mariners in navigating past treacherous Conimicut Point. The 23-foot brick tower was not built well and suffered much damage in an 1855 storm. The decision was made to rebuild and the current 25-foot, square tower was erected in 1856.

In 1868, a lighthouse was built at Conimicut Point and effectively put Nayatt Point Lighthouse out of service. Nayatt Point Lighthouse continued to serve as keeper's quarters, however, as the new beacon at Conimicut Point was not built with a living area. Eventually a new Conimicut Point Light was built with keeper's quarters and the Nayatt Point Lighthouse was sold at auction to a private owner in 1890. The 1828 house, Rhode Island's oldest keeper's quarters, is privately owned. The lighthouse is still operational and fitted with a lantern from a former lightship, but it is not currently used as a navigational aid.

Newport Harbor Light

**Contact Information:
The American Lighthouse Foundation
P.O. Box 889
Wells, Maine
(207) 646-0515
www.lighthousefoundation.com**

Latitude: 41° 29' 36" N
Longitude: 71° 19' 36" W

Newport Harbor Light

Also known as Goat Island Light
Newport, Rhode Island

Directions:
From RI 114 South in Newport: Turn right at Admiral Kalbfus Road. Then turn left at Third Street, then right at Sycamore Street (one way). Turn left at Washington Street, then turn right at the Goat Island Connector. Park at the Hyatt Hotel. The grounds of the lighthouse are accessible by passing through the lobby of the hotel. A good view is also possible from the lighthouse cruises offered periodically by Bay Queen Cruises in Warren, Rhode Island. Call Bay Queen cruises at (401) 245-1350 for details. Several other cruises in Newport offer views of the lighthouse, including M/V *Amazing Grace*, (401) 847-9109; *Spirit of Newport*, (401) 849-3575; Viking Tours of Newport, (401) 847-6921; and Yankee Boat Peddlers, (800) 427-9444.

Goat Island, primarily used as a military base for much of the nineteenth century, is home to Newport Harbor Light. A lighthouse was first established on the south end of the island in 1823, but it soon became evident that the location was ineffective and the light was too dim. In 1842, a new breakwater was built on the north end of the island and equipped with a 35-foot octagonal granite lighthouse. The original lighthouse was moved to Prudence Island, where it still stands.

A fourth-order Fresnel was installed in 1857 and exhibited a fixed green light visible for up to 11 nautical miles. A keeper's house was added to the new light in 1865 and a fog bell was added to the structure eight years later. Newport Harbor Light was electrified in 1922, one year before the keeper's house was damaged by a naval torpedo boat and demolished.

Today the light, which was automated in 1963, is located adjacent to the grounds of the Hyatt Regency Newport and can be accessed by walking through the hotel. Since 2000, the Newport Harbor Light has been leased by the American Lighthouse Foundation.

North Light

Latitude: 41° 13' 42" N
Longitude: 71° 34' 36" W

**North Light Fund
P.O. Box 1183
Block Island, Rhode Island 02807
Website:
www.angelfire.com/stars/richardrrg/
TheNorthLightFund.htm**

Block Island, a popular Rhode Island vacation spot, has also been the site of several shipwrecks. The frequent fog and dangerous shoals in the area have been the source of trouble for many mariners over the years. Between 1819 and 1839, 59 vessels were stranded or wrecked on the island.

A lighthouse was first commissioned on the sand bar known as Sandy Point in 1829. Known as Sandy Point Light, the 45-foot granite structure with twin beacons was threatened by erosion due to its unstable location. A second twin light was built in 1837 further inland, but this light was found to be ineffective due to its distance from the shore. Sandy Point Light was rebuilt as a single tower in 1857, but again fell victim to erosion.

North Light

Block Island, Rhode Island

Directions:
Block Island can be reached by ferry from Point Judith, Rhode Island; New London, Connecticut; and Montauk, New York. For information on the Point Judith and New London ferries call Interstate Navigation at (401) 783-4613. For information on the Montauk ferry, call Viking Fleet Ferry Lines at (516) 668-5700. You can also fly to Block Island via New England Airlines from Westerly (RI) Airport; call (800) 243-2460 for information. Block Island North Light is a few miles from the ferry landing. Bicycle rentals are available and taxis are usually in the vicinity of the ferry. If you bring your car: leave the ferry and turn right on Water Street. Follow onto Dodge Street. Turn right at Corn Neck Road and follow to the free parking area at the end of the road. The lighthouse is about a .05-mile walk on the sandy beach.

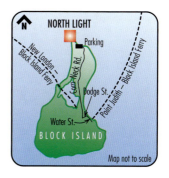

In 1867, North Light, affectionately known as "Old Granitesides," became the fourth light to be built on Sandy Point. Unlike the previous towers, North Light was built with a solid concrete foundation to avoid the forces of erosion. The two-and-one-half-story, Victorian-style keeper's quarters and iron tower was built 700 yards inland and fitted with a fourth-order Fresnel that exhibited a fixed white light visible from 13 miles at sea. The optic was later changed to a flashing white light and was electrified in the 1940s.

Although deactivated in 1973 and replaced with an offshore skeleton tower, North Light remained a popular tourist attraction for Block Island visitors. The area became part of a wildlife refuge known for its flourishing bird community. Residents soon began to petition for a relighting of the beacon and North Light was reactivated on August 5, 1989. The lighthouse now serves as an active aid to navigation and a museum. Plans are underway to restore the upper floors of the lighthouse and convert the light to wind power.

Plum Beach Light

Latitude: 41° 31' 49" N
Longitude: 71° 24' 19" W

**Contact Information:
The Friends of Plum Beach Lighthouse, Inc.
P.O. Box 451
Portsmouth, RI 02871**

Plum Beach Light

North Kingstown, Rhode Island

Directions:
Travel west on RI 138 in Jamestown and take the exit marked North Main Street. Turn left at Frigate Street, and left again at Beacon Street. Turn right at Pickering Street, left at Helm Street, and right at Spindrift Street. The lighthouse can be seen from the end of Spindrift Street. A good view is also possible from the lighthouse cruises offered periodically by Bay Queen Cruises in Warren, Rhode Island. Call Bay Queen cruises at (401) 245-1350 for details.

Plum Beach Light, built in the west passage of the Narragansett Bay, was built at the request of ship captains who detoured Dutch Island in dense fog. Due to the stormy weather and choppy water in the area, the caisson-supported tower was a challenge to construct and was not completed until June 1899. In the meantime, a temporary red lantern and fog bell were installed to guide ships traveling in the area.

The 53-foot white conical tower was first fitted with a fourth-order Fresnel that flashed a white beam every five seconds. Plum Beach Light survived several severe winters and, more impressively, the Hurricane of 1938, which destroyed many Rhode Island lighthouses and killed 262 people in the area.

In 1941, upon completion of the Jamestown Bridge, Plum Beach Light was rendered obsolete and decommissioned. For several years, the lighthouse suffered neglect as the U.S. Coast Guard and the state of Rhode Island argued about who owned the structure. In 1998, the government ruled that the state owned the light. One year later, the property was purchased by the nonprofit group The Friends of Plum Beach Lighthouse, who began restoration on the lighthouse in the summer of 2002.

Point Judith Lighthouse

Latitude: 41° 21' 42" N
Longitude: 71° 28' 54" W

Although a formal lighthouse was not built on this spot until 1810, a day beacon had been installed at the busy shipping harbor of Point Judith before the American Revolution to mark the mile-long shoal that protrudes from the Rhode Island coast between Block Island Sound and Narragansett Bay.

The original light at Point Judith, built of wood at a cost of $5,000, was destroyed in an 1815 storm. A 35-foot granite lighthouse with a revolving light replaced the original the following year. Unfortunately, shipwrecks continued to occur in the area, and the lighthouse was demolished and replaced with the current 51-foot brownstone tower in 1857.

Point Judith Lighthouse

Narragansett, Rhode Island

Directions:
From US Route 1 in Wakefield, take the exit for RI 108 south to Point Judith. The road terminates at a four-way stop. Turn right onto Ocean Road and follow to the light station. The grounds are open daily and there is free parking.

In 1931, Point Judith Lighthouse made history when it became the first station in Rhode Island to have a radio beacon, which allowed vessels to navigate at night or in stormy weather without relying on the light or foghorn to guide them. The octagonal structure, equipped with a fourth-order Fresnel lens that exhibits a flashing white light, continues to serve Point Judith's busy harbor today, although the light was automated in 1954. A U.S. Coast Guard station was built adjacent to the lighthouse in 1937, and while the 1857 keeper's house has been demolished, the light's original 1917 oil house and 1923 fog-signal building still stand.

Point Judith Lighthouse underwent a major restoration in the summer of 2000, when the Coast Guard spent approximately $250,000 renovating the historic tower and lantern room. Visitors can walk the refurbished light's grounds today, although the lighthouse itself is not open to the public.

Pomham Rocks Lighthouse

Latitude: 41° 46' 36" N
Longitude: 71° 22' 12" W

The light at Pomham Rocks, named for a Narragansett Indian chief who fought in King Philip's War and was killed in 1676, was first lit on December 1, 1871. The two-story, French Second Empire-style house was built with an adjoining light tower that held a sixth-order Fresnel lens.

A fog siren was added in 1900. Local residents, however, complained of the continuous noise and the horn was replaced three years later by a fog bell. In 1939, Pomham Rocks Light's sixth-order Fresnel was upgraded to a

Pomham Rocks Lighthouse

East Providence, Rhode Island

Directions: Pomham Rocks Lighthouse can be easily seen from the East Bay Bicycle Path in East Providence. The path is open to walkers as well as bikers. It extends from Bristol to Providence. To reach the parking area closest to the lighthouse: Head east on I-195, take exit 4, Riverside/Veteran's Memorial Parkway (RI 103). Continue about 5 miles to the Bullocks Point Road parking area to reach the bike path. The view of the lighthouse is a short walk to the north.

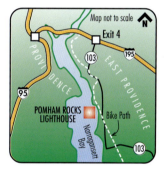

fourth-order lens, which was subsequently removed upon the lighthouse's decommission in 1974 and put on display at the Custom House Maritime Museum in Newburyport, Massachusetts.

Pomham Rocks Light was sold to the neighboring Mobil Oil Company in 1980. Although the light is no longer functional, it is still cared for by the energy giant and can be viewed from the East Bay Bicycle Path.

Poplar Point Light

Latitude: 41° 34' 16" N
Longitude: 71° 26' 21" W

Poplar Point Light

Wickford, Rhode Island

Directions:
Poplar Point Light is best viewed from across Wickford Harbor at Sauga Point. From US Route 1 in Wickford, take Camp Avenue south. Turn right at Shore Acres Road. On Shore Acres there is a pathway marked with a "Private Property" sign. The path is actually a public walkthrough. Head down the lane to the beach, then walk west to a breakwater. From the breakwater, Poplar Point Light can be seen across the harbor.

The 48-foot wooden tower known as Poplar Point Light served as a navigational aid at the entrance of Wickford Harbor for only half a century. Built in 1831 for $3,000, the wooden, Cape Cod-style light originally held a series of eight lamps and 14.5-inch reflectors, which were replaced in 1855 by a fifth-order Fresnel lens.

In 1882, Poplar Point Light was put out of service by the more powerful Wickford Harbor Light. Poplar Point Light is the oldest surviving lighthouse in Rhode Island still on its original site, and it is believed to be the oldest original wooden lighthouse in the United States. The structure has been privately owned since 1894.

Rose Island Lighthouse

Latitude: 41° 29' 42" N
Longitude: 71° 20' 36" W

Contact Information:
Rose Island Lighthouse Foundation
P.O. Box 1419
Newport, Rhode Island 02840-0997
(401) 847-4242
www.roseislandlighthouse.com

This French Second Empire Revival-style lighthouse was built at the corner of Rose Island in 1870 to help mariners navigate the tricky east passage of Narragansett Bay. Before construction of the light, steamboat companies sent a man on a rowboat out to the spot to sound a fog signal in stormy

Rose Island Lighthouse

Newport, Rhode Island

Directions:
Rose Island Lighthouse can be seen distantly from various points on shore. The island is reached via the Jamestown-Newport ferry. The roundtrip fare is $12 for adults, and $6 for children between the ages of six and ten. Children must be accompanied by an adult. The ferry stops at Rose Island on request, and there is a $1 landing fee per person. The ferry leaves Goat Island Marina in Newport. Call (401) 423-9900 for ferry information. Rose Island Light can also be viewed from several harbor tours leaving Newport, including M/V *Amazing Grace*, (401) 847 9109; *Spirit of Newport*, (401) 849-3575; Viking Tours of Newport, (401) 847-6921; and Yankee Boat Peddlers, (401) 847-0298 or (800) 427-9444.

weather as a warning to approaching vessels. Rose Island Lighthouse's sixth-order Fresnel lens was first lit on January 20, 1870 and exhibited a fixed red light. A fog bell was added fifteen years later. Rose Island was part of the Naval Torpedo Station in the twentieth century, and explosives were stored in the island's partially built Fort Hamilton during World War I and World War II. After the second world war, the military sold its property on the island and abandoned the area. This left it open to vandalism, which became worse in 1971 when the Newport bridge was built and Rose Island Lighthouse was decommissioned.

After a stint as a marine research station for the University of Rhode Island, Rose Island Lighthouse was purchased by a group of citizens who formed the Rose Island Lighthouse Foundation. In 1984, the group took over the historic property and began to restore it to its former glory. On August 7, 1993, Rose Island Lighthouse was relit. Guests who want a true taste of "keeper life" can reside at the lighthouse for overnight or weeklong stays. During these visits, guests raise the flag, record the weather and other data, and perform general maintenance chores.

Sakonnet Point Lighthouse

**Contact Information:
The Friends of Sakonnet Point Lighthouse, Inc.
P.O. Box 154
Little Compton, Rhode Island**

Latitude: 41° 27' 12" N
Longitude: 71° 12' 12" W

Sakonnet Point Lighthouse

Sakonnet, Rhode Island

Directions:
Travel south on RI 77 in Tiverton until you reach its terminus near the beach in Little Compton. There is a free parking area. On the left, just before the beach parking area, walk down a narrow paved lane to a walled beach overlook. In summer, the beach is open to residents only, but you can see the lighthouse from the overlook, about six-tenths of a mile away.

On the east side of the Sakonnet River is Little Cormorant Rock. It is here that Sakonnet Point Lighthouse was established in October 1884, after nearly a year of construction. The white, conical lighthouse equipped with a fourth-order Fresnel lens is Rhode Island's easternmost beacon. Over the years, the 66-foot tower weathered many storms, including the Hurricane of 1938 and Hurricane Carol in 1954. Though no keepers were ever injured as a result of the storms, the powerful elements took their toll on the brick-lined iron tower.

Sakonnet Point Lighthouse was decommissioned in 1954 and sold to a private owner at auction. In 1985, the lighthouse was donated to The Friends of Sakonnet Point Lighthouse, Inc., a nonprofit organization dedicated to raising funds for the restoration of the beacon. After extensive renovation, the tower was equipped with a modern optic that exhibits a red flash every six seconds and was relit on March 22, 1997.

The light continues to serve as an active aid to navigation and can be seen up to seven miles at sea.

Sandy Point Lighthouse
Latitude: 41° 36' 36" N
Longitude: 71° 18' 12" W

Contact Information:
Prudence Conservancy
P.O. Box 115
Prudence Island, Rhode Island 02872

Sandy Point Lighthouse

Also known as Prudence Island Lighthouse
Prudence Island, Rhode Island

Directions:
Prudence Island can be reached via car/passenger ferry (crossing time is about 20 minutes) from Bristol's Church Street Wharf. From RI 114 in Bristol, take any cross street to Thames Street. The wharf is at the intersection of Thames and Church Streets. Call (401) 253-9808 for ferry information. From the ferry dock on Prudence Island, the lighthouse is approximately a 1-mile walk. Head left from the ferry dock. There are no restaurants on Prudence Island, so plan accordingly. The lighthouse can also be viewed from the occasional lighthouse cruises offered by Bay Queen Cruises in Warren, Rhode Island. Call Bay Queen cruises at (401) 245-1350 for details.

Sandy Point Lighthouse originally stood on Newport Harbor's Goat Island. The 25-foot granite tower was relocated to Sandy Point, located on Prudence Island, in 1851 and lit in 1852. A fifth-order Fresnel replaced the beacon's earlier lighting system in 1857 and a fog bell was added in 1885. Sandy Point Lighthouse was upgraded to a fourth-order Fresnel in 1939 and electrified. Twenty-two years later, the structure was automated.

The keeper's house was destroyed in one of the worst disasters in the lighthouse's history. During the Hurricane of 1938, the building was swept away, killing keeper George Gustavus's wife, son, and three others. Gustavus himself was swept into the sea, but was carried back onto shore moments later. After the storm, Gustavus resigned from his post as keeper and never returned to the lighthouse.

Sandy Point Lighthouse still serves as an active aid to navigation and is now fitted with a 250-millimeter modern lens. The light, though not open to the public, is accessible to visitors who take a ferry from Bristol. The lighthouse is approximately a 1-mile walk from the ferry port.

Southeast Light

**Contact Information:
Block Island Southeast
Lighthouse Foundation
Box 949
Block Island, RI 02807
(401) 466-5009**

Latitude: 41° 09' 12" N
Longitude: 71° 33' 06" W

Southeast Light, the highest light in New England, was built as an accompaniment to Block Island's North Light. In 1856, the government issued $9,000 for the construction of a lighthouse at the southeast tip of Block Island. The money was instead used to repair the existing North Light and Southeast Light was forgotten until 1872, when a local merchant started a petition to have a lighthouse built on the spot. T.H. Tynan of State Island served as the construction company for the Italianate/Gothic Revival-style light.

The completed light was one of the grandest in the nation, with an attached brick keeper's house standing tall at two-and-a-half stories. Other buildings included a garage, a storage building, a boathouse, and an oil house. The octagonal tower was installed with a first-order Fresnel lens, which was first lit on February 1, 1875.

Southeast Light

Block Island, Rhode Island

Directions:
Block Island can be reached by ferry from Point Judith, Rhode Island; New London, Connecticut; and Montauk, New York. For information on the Point Judith and New London ferries call Interstate Navigation at (401) 783-4613. For information on the Montauk ferry, call Viking Fleet Ferry Lines at (516) 668-5700. You can also fly to Block Island via New England Airlines from Westerly (RI) Airport; call (800) 243-2460 or (401) 596-2460 for information. Block Island Holidays offers a wide range of tour packages and activies on the island; call (800) 905-0590 or (401) 466-3115. From the ferry, walk to the road and turn left; Block Island Southeast Light is about a 30-minute walk (some of it uphill). Taxis are readily available in the area near the ferry.

In 1929, the light was changed to a flashing green beacon to help sailors differentiate it from other lights in the area. During the Hurricane of 1938, which wrecked the house's radio beacon and oil house and destroyed all power connections, keepers were forced to turn the lens by hand for several days. The present electric fog signal was added in 1974.

In 1990, the Coast Guard deactivated the light and replaced it with a steel skeleton tower. Over the years, erosion had crept up on the light, leaving it standing a mere 55 feet from the edge of the island. The light soon was on the National Trust for Historic Preservation's list of most endangered historic structures. Thanks to a group of volunteers who started the Block Island Southeast Lighthouse Foundation, the light was moved in August 1993 to its current location about 300 feet from the edge of the bluffs. The group restored the light and efforts to relight the beacon were rewarded on August 27, 1994.

Southeast Lighthouse is now home to a small museum and gift shop. Tours of the structure are available throughout the summer.

Warwick Light

Latitude: 41° 40' 00" N
Longitude: 71° 22' 42" W

Warwick Light

Warwick, Rhode Island

Directions:
From US Route 1 North: Turn right onto RI 117, then right again at Warwick Neck Avenue. Continue south to the light station. Visitors are not admitted into the station, and the view from the gate is partly blocked. A good view from the water is available from the lighthouse cruises offered periodically by Bay Queen Cruises in Warren, Rhode Island. Call Bay Queen cruises at (401) 245-1350 for details.

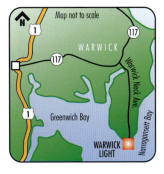

Warwick Light was first established in 1826. The 30-foot tower was originally attached to the roof of a two-room stone building. The house's keeper complained that the house was too cramped and damp, and the original house was replaced with a three-room wooden house in 1831. The new quarters were replaced with a Victorian dwelling in 1889 and the former wooden keeper's house was converted to a barn.

In 1932, the lighthouse was torn down after years of being threatened by erosion and a new 51-foot steel tower with an electric light was built on the site. This beacon flashes a green beam every four seconds and continues to serve as an active aid to navigation for the United States Coast Guard.

Watch Hill Lighthouse

**Contact Information:
Watch Hill Lighthouse
Keepers Assocation
14 Lighthouse Road
Watch Hill, RI 02891**

Latitude: 41° 18' 12" N
Longitude: 71° 34' 30" W

Watch Hill Lighthouse

Westerly, Rhode Island

Directions:
From RI 1A North or South: Turn south onto Watch Hill Road, which will eventually bear slightly right onto Wauwinnett Road. Bear left onto connecting Bay Street. Turn left at Larkin Road. Just before Bluff Road on the right is Lighthouse Road; a paved lane leads to the lighthouse station. Seniors (64+) and the handicapped are permitted to drive to the parking area near the station. Others must park outside of Lighthouse Road and walk to the lighthouse.

Watch Hill Tower receives its name from the watch tower and beacon that were established here as early as 1745. The decision to build a lighthouse here to mark the eastern entrance to Fishers Island Sound was approved in 1806 by President Thomas Jefferson.

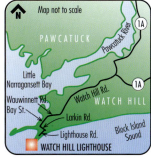

The first beacon on the spot was a 35-foot, round, wooden tower with ten whale oil lamps and reflectors. Erosion eventually threatened the tower and a new structure was built further inland in 1856. The new tower was 45 feet tall and lined with brick. Its fourth-order Fresnel lens emitted a fixed white light. A two-story keeper's house and protective sea wall were also built during this time.

After the steamer *Metis* sunk near Watch Hill in 1872, killing over 100 passengers, a United States Life Saving Service Station was established near the lighthouse. The station was abandoned in the 1940s and demolished in 1963.

In 1986, Watch Hill Lighthouse became automated and the Fresnel lens was replaced with a modern optic. Watch Hill Lighthouse continues to serve as an active aid to navigation and today is home to a museum that is open to the public for limited hours in the summer. The light's original fourth-order Fresnel lens is on display in the museum. Watch Hill Lighthouse is run by the Watch Hill Lighthouse Keepers Association, which is in charge of the station's upkeep. The group has hired a resident keeper for the light.

Appendix

EDITOR'S NOTE: All of the events listed in this appendix are for 2003 only and were gathered from various sources, including the Connecticut Vacation Guide and Rhode Island Official Travel Guide. Please call to verify correct information and dates.

2003 Connecticut Calendar of Events

February
20–23   Connecticut Flower and Garden Show, Hartford (860-529-2123, www.northeastpromo.com)

April
14–May 4   Goldenbells Festival, Hamden (goldenbellsfestival@aol.com). Calendar of events available at Hamden public library, town hall, and schools.
26–27   Daffodil Festival, Meriden (203-630-4259, www.daffodilfest.com)

May
17   Sound Winds Kite Festival, Madison (860-344-6200, www.soundwinds.org)
17–18   Meet the Artists and Artisans, Milford (features lots of lighthouse art, 203-874-5672, www.artistsandartisans.bizland.com)
23–26   Lime Rock Park Grand Prix, Lakeville (800-RACE-LRP, www.limerock.com)
24–26   Lobsterfest, Mystic (888-9-SEAPORT, www.mysticseaport.org)

June
TBA   International Festival of Arts & Ideas, New Haven (888-ART-IDEA, www.artidea.org)
14–15   Farmington Antiques Weekend, Farmington (317-598-0019, www.farmington-antiques.com)
21–27   Greater Hartford Open PGA Event, Cromwell (888-CANON-GHO, www.canongho.com)

July
2   Fourth of July Festival, Norwich (860-886-6363)
3–6   Subfest, Groton (860-694-3238)
4–6   Fourth of July Town Celebration, Enfield (860-749-1820, www.enfieldcelebration.org)
6   Riverfest, Hartford/East Hartford (860-713-3131, www.riverfront.org)
11–13   Sailfest, New London (860-444-1879, www.sailfest.org)
12   Mashantucket Pequot Thames River Fireworks, Groton/New London (860-443-1980)
17–19   Guilford Handcrafts Exposition, Guilford (203-453-5947, www.handcraftcenter.org)
24–27   Great Connecticut Jazz Festival, Guilford (800-HOT-EVENT, www.ctjazz.org)
26–27   Antique & Classic Boat Rendezvous, Mystic (888-9-SEAPORT, www.mysticseaport.org)
26–27   Meet the Artists and Artisans, Mystic (203-874-5672, www.artistsandartisans.bizland.com)

August

1–3	Litchfield Jazz Festival, Goshen (860-567-4162, www.litchfieldjazzfest.com)
8–9	Mystic Outdoor Art Festival, Mystic (860-572-9578, www.mysticchamber.org/indmoaf.html)
15–23	Pilot Pen Tennis Women's Championships, New Haven (888-99-PILOT, www.pilotpentennis.com)
29–31	Mark Twain Days, Hartford (860-713-3131, www.marktwaindays.org)
29–Sept. 1	Woodstock Fair, South Woodstock (860-928-3246, www.woodstockfair.com)
30–31	Farmington Antiques Weekend, Farmington (317-598-0019, www.farmington-antiques.com)
30–Sept. 1	Meet the Artists and Artisans, Mystic (203-874-5672, www.artistsandartisans.bizland.com)

September

5–7	Bethlehem Fair, Bethlehem (203-266-5350, www.bethlehemfair.com)
5–7	Norwalk Oyster Festival, East Norwalk (203-838-9444, www.seaport.org)
5–7	Boats, Books & Brushes, New London (860-443-8332, www.sailnewlondon.com)
11–14	Four Town Fair, Somers (860-749-6527)
26–28	Durham Fair, Durham (860-349-9495, www.durhamfair.com)
27–28	Meet the Artists and Artisans, Milford (203-874-5672, www.artistsandartisans.bizland.com)

October

3–5	Berlin Fair, Berlin (860-828-0063)
4–5, 9–12	Apple Harvest Festival, Southington (860-628-8036)
11	Greater Hartford Marathon, Hartford (860-652-8866, www.hartfordmarathon.com)
11–13	Chowderfest, Mystic (888-9-SEAPORT, www.mysticseaport.org)
11–13	Walking Weekend, Northeast Connecticut (860-963-7226)

November

7–Dec. 30	Holiday Craft Exhibition and Sale, Brookfield (203-775-4526)
22	Stamford Parade Spectacular, Stamford (203-348-5285)
26–Jan. 4	Holiday Light Fantasia, Hartford (860-343-1565)
27	Manchester Road Race, Manchester (860-649-6456, www.manchesterroadrace.com)
29–Dec. 13	Wesleyan Potters Exhibit & Sale, Middletown (860-347-5925, www.wesleyanpotters.com)

December

4–21	Lantern Light Tours, Mystic (888-9-SEAPORT, www.mysticseaport.org)
6–7	Holidayfest, North Central Connecticut (800-248-8283)
31	First Night Hartford, Hartford (860-722-9546, www.firstnighthartford.com)

Accommodations in Connecticut

Bridgeport (Fayerweather Island Light/Tongue Point Light)
Other Sites of Interest:
The Barnum Museum, Bridgeport, (203) 331-1104
Beardsley Zoological Gardens, Bridgeport, (203) 394-6565
Captain's Cove Seaport, Bridgeport, (203) 335-1433
The Discovery Museum, Bridgeport, (203) 372-3521
Housatonic Museum of Art, Bridgeport, (203) 332-5000

Accommodations:
Bridgeport Holiday Inn, Bridgeport, (203) 334-1234

Fairfield (Penfield Reef Light)
Other Sites of Interest:
Connecticut Audubon Birdcraft Museum, Fairfield, (203) 259-0416
Connecticut Audubon Center at Fairfield, Fairfield, (203) 259-6305
Ogden House and Gardens, Fairfield, (203) 259-1598
Walsh Art Gallery, Fairfield, (203) 254-4000

Accommodations:
Fairfield Inn, Fairfield, (203) 255-0491
Merritt Parkway Motor Inn, Fairfield, (203) 259-5264
Seagrape Inn, Fairfield, (203) 255-6808

Greenwich (Great Captain Island Lighthouse)
Other Sites of Interest:
Audubon Center in Greenwich, Greenwich, (203) 869-5272
Bruce Museum of Arts & Science, Greenwich, (203) 869-0376
Bush-Holley Historic Site & Visitor Center, Greenwich, (203) 869-6899
Putnam Cottage, Greenwich, (203) 869-9697

Accommodations:
Cos Cob Inn, Greenwich, (203) 661-5845
DELAMAR Greenwich Harbor, Greenwich, (203) 661-9800
Howard Johnson Greenwich Hotel, Greenwich, (203) 637-3691
Stanton House Inn, Greenwich, (203) 869-2110

Groton (Avery Point Lighthouse)
Other Sites of Interest:
Fort Griswold Battlefield State Park, Groton, (860) 445-1729
Historic Ship *Nautilus* and Submarine Force Museum, Groton, (860) 694-3174
U.S. Submarine World War II Veteran's Memorial (East), Groton, (860) 399-8666

Accommodations:
Benham Motel, Groton, (860) 449-5700
Bestway Inn and Suites, Groton, (800) 280-0054
Clarion Inn, Groton, (860) 446-0660

Mystic Marriott Hotel & Spa, Groton, (860) 446-2600
Thames Inn and Marina, Groton, (860) 445-8111

Guilford (Faulkners Island Light)
Other Sites of Interest:
Dudley Farm, Guilford, (203) 457-0770
Hammonasset Beach State Park, Madison, (203) 245-2785
Henry Whitfield State Museum, Guilford, (203) 453-2457
The Sculpture Mile, Madison, (860) 767-2624
Thomas Griswold House, Guilford, (203) 453-3176

Accommodations:
Guilford Suites Hotel, Guilford, (203) 453-0123
Guilford Corners B&B, Guilford, (203) 453-4129
Madison Beach Hotel, Madison, (203) 245-1404
Tidewater Inn B&B, Madison, (203) 245-8457
Tower Suites Motel, Guilford, (203) 453-9069

Mystic/Noank (Mystic Seaport Lighthouse/Morgan Point Lighthouse)
Other Sites of Interest:
Denison Homestead Museum/Pequotsepos Manor, Mystic, (860) 536-9248
Haight Winery, Mystic, (860) 572-1978
Mystic Aquarium and Institute for Exploration, Mystic, (860) 572-5955
Mystic Seaport, Mystic, (860) 572-5315
Olde Mistick Village, Mystic, (860) 536-4941

Accommodations:
Adams House of Mystic, Mystic, (860) 572-9551
Comfort Inn of Mystic, Mystic, (860) 572-8531
Harbour Inne & Cottage, Mystic, (860) 572-9253
Old Mystic Motor Lodge, Mystic, (860) 536-9666
Whitehall Mansion, Mystic, (860) 572-7280

New Haven (Five Mile Point Lighthouse/Southwest Ledge Light)
Other Sites of Interest:
Connecticut Children's Museum, New Haven, (203) 562-5437
Edgewood Park, New Haven, (203) 946-8028
Knights of Columbus Museum, New Haven, (203) 865-0400
Peabody Museum of Natural History, New Haven, (203) 432-5050
Yale University Visitor Information Center, New Haven, (203) 432-2300

Accommodations:
Colony Inn, New Haven, (203) 776-1234
The Inn at Oyster Point, New Haven, (203) 773-3334
New Haven Hotel, New Haven, (203) 498-3100
Swan Cove B&B, New Haven, (203) 776-3240
Touch of Ireland Guest House, (203) 787-7997

New London (New London Ledge Lighthouse/New London Harbor Lighthouse)
Other Sites of Interest:
Connecticut College Arboretum, New London, (860) 439-5020
Lyman Allyn Art Museum, New London, (860) 443-2545
Monte Cristo Cottage, New London, (860) 443-0051
Science Center of Eastern Connecticut, New London, (860) 442-0391
U.S. Coast Guard Academy, New London, (860) 444-8270

Accommodations:
Holiday Inn, New London, (860) 442-0631
Lighthouse Inn, New London, (860) 443-8411
New London Lodgings, New London, (860) 443-3440
Queen Anne Inn, New London, (860) 447-2600
Red Roof Inn, New London, (860) 444-0001

Norwalk (Greens Ledge Light/Peck Ledge Light/Sheffield Island Light)
Other Sites of Interest:
Connecticut GraphicArts Center, Norwalk, (203) 899-7999
Lockwood-Mathews Mansion Museum, Norwalk, (203) 838-9799
The Maritime Aquarium at Norwalk, Norwalk, (203) 852-0700
Stepping Stones Museum for Children, Norwalk, (203) 899-0606
WPA Murals, Norwalk, (203) 866-0202

Accommodations:
Courtyard by Marriott, Norwalk, (203) 849-9111
Garden Park Motel, Norwalk, (203) 847-7303
Homestead Studio Suites Hotel, Norwalk, (203) 847-6888
Round Tree Inn, Norwalk, (203) 847-5827
Silvermine Tavern, Norwalk, (203) 847-4558

Old Saybrook (Lynde Point Light/Saybrook Breakwater Lighthouse)
Other Sites of Interest:
Florence Griswold Museum, Old Lyme, (860) 434-5542
Fort Saybrook Monument Park, Old Saybrook, (860) 395-3123
General William Hart House, Old Saybrook, (860) 395-1635
Military Historians Museum, Westbrook, (860) 399-9460
Westbrook Factory Outlets, Westbrook, (860) 399-8656

Accommodations:
Beach Plum Inn, Westbrook, (860) 399-9345
Bee & Thistle Inn, Old Lyme, (860) 434-1667
Captain Stannard House, Westbrook, (860) 399-4634
Liberty Inn, Old Saybrook, (860) 388-1777
Saybrook Point Inn and Spa, Old Saybrook, (860) 395-2000
 Resort, Westbrook, (860) 399-5901

 amford Harbor Light)
 Interest:
 retum, Stamford, (203) 322-6971

Bruce Museum of Arts & Science, Greenwich, (203) 869-0376
Stamford Museum & Nature Center, Stamford, (203) 322-1646
United House Wrecking Company Antiques, Stamford, (203) 348-5371

Accommodations:
Budget Hospitality Inn, Stamford, (203) 327-4300
Holiday Inn Select, Stamford, (203) 358-8400
Stamford Motor Lodge, Stamford, (203) 325-2655
Stamford Suites Hotel, Stamford, (203) 359-7300
The Westin Stamford, Stamford, (203) 967-2222

Stonington (Stonington Harbor Lighthouse)
Other Sites of Interest:
Captain Nathaniel B. Palmer House, Stonington, (860) 535-8445
Jonathan Edwards Winery, North Stonington, (860) 535-0202
Maple Breeze Amusement Park, Pawcatuck, (860) 599-1232
Stonington Vineyards, Stonington, (860) 535-1222

Accommodations:
Antiques & Accommodations, North Stonington, (860) 535-1736
Cove Ledge Inn & Marina, Stonington, (860) 599-4130
The John York House B&B, North Stonington, (860) 599-3075
Stardust Motel, North Stonington, (860) 599-2261
Stonington Motel, Stonington, (860) 599-2330

Stratford (Stratford Point Lighthouse/Stratford Shoal Light)
Other Sites of Interest:
The Barnum Museum, Bridgeport, (203) 331-1104
Boothe Memorial Park & Museum, Stratford, (203) 381-2046
Connecticut Audubon Coastal Center, Milford, (203) 878-7440
The Garbage Museum, Stratford, (203) 381-9571
Stratford Antique Center, Stratford, (203) 378-7754

Accommodations:
Marnick's Restaurant-Motel, Stratford, (203) 377-6288
Mayflower Motel, Milford, (203) 878-6854
Nathan Booth House B&B, Stratford, (203) 378-6489
Staybridge Suites by Holiday Inn, Stratford, (203) 377-3322
Trumbull Marriott, Trumbull, (203) 378-1400

2003 Rhode Island Calendar of Events

January
1	Jamestown Penguin Plunge, Jamestown (401-823-7411, www.gonewport.com)
10–12	A Celebration of Twelfth Night, Westerly (401-596-8663, www.chorusofwesterly.org)

February
14–23   Newport Winter Festival, Newport
         (401-847-7666, www.newportevents.com)

March
1–31   Irish Heritage Month, Newport
         (401-845-9123, www.gonewport.com)
15   St. Patrick's Day Parade, Newport
         (401-845-9123, www.gonewport.com)

April
7   Pawtucket Red Sox Opening Day, Pawtucket
         (401-724-7300, www.pawsox.com)
12–30   Daffodil Days, Bristol (401-253-2707, www.blithewold.org)
19   Easter Egg Hunt of Rosecliff Mansion, Newport
         (401-847-1000, www.newportmansions.com)
26   Pawtucket River Duck Race, Pawtucket
         (401-596-7761, www.westerlychamber.org)

May
16–18   Newport Fun Cup Windsurfing Regatta, Newport
         (401-846-4421, www.islandsports.com/funcup)
17   Fort Adams Opening Day, Newport
         (401-841-0707, www.fortadams.org)
17   Sail Newport/Bank of Newport Family Sailing Festival, Newport
         (401-846-1983, www.sailnewport.org)
18   Chorus of Westerly Spring Concert
         (401-596-8663, www.chorusofwesterly.org)
24–25   "Virtu" Art Festival, Westerly
         (401-596-7761, www.westerlychamber.org)
24–26   Gaspee Days Arts and Crafts Festival, Warwick
         (401-781-1772, www.gaspee.com)

June
May 30–1 Newport Spring Boat Show, Newport
         (401-846-1115, www.newportexhibition.com)
7   Festival of Historic Houses Candlelight Tour, Providence
         (401-831-7440, www.ppsri.org)
7–8   Snug Harbor June Moon Madness Striper Tournament, Wakefield
         (401-783-7766, www.snugharbormarina.com)
10–15   Newport International Film Festival, Newport
         (www.newportfilmfestival.com)
14   Gaspee Days Parade, Warwick (401-781-1772, www.gaspee.com)
21–22   Narragansett Art Festival, Wakefield
         (401-783-1820, www.wakefieldrotary.com)
28   Rhode Island National Guard Open House and Air Show,
         North Kingstown (401-275-4060,
         www.riguard.com/airshow.html)

July

1–6	Sunset Musical Festival, Newport, (401-846-1600, www.newportfestivals.com)
4	Bristol Fourth of July Parade, Bristol (401-253-0445, www.July4thbristolri.com)
7–13	Miller Lite Hall of Fame Championship, Newport, (401-849-6053, www.tennisfame.com)
12–13	Snug Harbor Shark Tournament, Wakefield, (401-783-7766, www.snugharbormarina.com)
12–13	Wickford Art Festival, North Kingstown (401-294-6480, www.wickfordart.org)
17–20	Black Ships Festival, Newport, (401-846-2720, wwww.newportevents.com)

August

TBA	Fools' Rules Regatta, Jamestown (401-423-1492, www.jyc.org)
8–10	JVC Jazz Festival, Newport (401-847-3700, www.festivalproductions.net)
9–10	Narragansett Indian Pow Wow, Charlestown (401-364-1100, www.narragansett-tribe.org)
15–16	Volvo Leukemia Cup Regatta, Bristol (401-943-8888, www.leukemia-lymphoma.org)
15–17	Newport Folk Festival, Newport (401-847-3700, www.newportfolk.com)
23–24	International Quahog Festival, Wickford (401-885-4118, www.quahog.com)
29-31	Rhythm and Roots Festival, Charlestown, (888-855-6940, www.rhythmandroots.com)
29–31	Classic Yacht Regatta and Parade, Newport (401-847-1018, www.moy.org)
31	Around the Island Race, Jamestown, (401-423-1424, www.conanicutyachtclub.org)

September

5–21	Convergence International Arts Festival (401-621-1992, www.caparts.org)
11–14	Newport International Boat Show, Newport (401-846-1115, www.newportboatshow.com)
27–28	Aquafina Taste of Rhode Island, Newport (401-846-1600, www.newportfestivals.com)

October

TBA	Block Island Birding Weekend, Block Island (401-949-5454, www.asri.org)
TBA	Jack O'Lantern Spectacular, Providence (401-785-3510, www.rogerwilliamsparkzoo.org)
11–13	Scituate Art Festival, North Scituate (401-647-0057, www.scituateartfestival.org)

October - *continued*

11–13	NBC-10 Oktoberfest, Newport (401-846-1600, www.newportfestivals.com)
11–13	Woonsocket Autumnfest, Woonsocket (401-762-9072, www.autumnfest.org)
12	Ocean State Marathon, Warwick to Providence (401-885-4499 www.osm26.com)
18–19	Bowen's Wharf Seafood Festival, Newport (401-849-2120, www.bowenswharf.com)
23–26	RIIFF Horror Film Festival, Providence (401-861-4445, www.film-festival.org)

November

1	Guy Fawkes Bonfire, Misquamicut (401-596-9441, www.misquamicut.org)
7-9	Fine Furnishings Show, Providence (401-846-1115, www.finefurnishingsshow.com)
29–Jan. 1	Christmas at the Newport Mansions, Newport (401-847-1000, www.newportmansions.org)
TBA	Christmas in Newport, Newport (401-849-6454, www.christmasinnewport.org)
TBA	Festival of Lights, North Kingstown (401-295-5566)
TBA	Christmas at Blithewold, Bristol (401-253-2707, www.blithewold.org)

December

31	First Night Providence, Providence (401-521-1166, www.firstnightprovidence.org)
31	Opening Night, Newport (401-848-2400)

Accommodations in Rhode Island

Barrington (Nayatt Point Lighthouse)
Other Sites of Interest:
Bay Queen Cruises, Warren, (401-245-1350)
Blithewold Mansion and Gardens, Bristol, (401-253-2707)
Haffenreffer Museum of Anthropology, Bristol, (401-253-8388)
Mount Hope Farm, Bristol, (401-254-1745)
Preservation Society Museum, Barrington, (401-247-3770)

Accommodations:
Bristol Harbor Inn, Bristol, (401-254-1444)
Candlewick Inn, Warren, (401-247-2425)
Hearth House, Bristol, (401-253-1404)
Nathaniel Porter Inn, Warren, (401-245-6622)
Thomas Cole House, Warren, (401-245-9768)

Block Island (North Light/ Southeast Light)
Other Sites of Interest:
Block Island Historical Society, New Shoreham, (401-466-2481)
Manisses Animal Farm, New Shoreham, (401-466-2421)
Rodman's Hollow, New Shoreham, (401-466-2129)

Accommodations:
The 1661 Inn and Hotel Manisses, New Shoreham, (401-466-2421)
Harbourview Cottages, New Shoreham, (401-466-2807)
Hygeia House, New Shoreham, (401-466-9616)
The National Hotel, New Shoreham, (401-466-2901)
Rose Farm Inn, New Shoreham, (401-466-2034)

Bristol (Bristol Ferry Light)
Other Sites of Interest:
Audubon Society of Rhode Island's Environmental Education Center, Bristol, (401-245-7500)
Blithewold Mansion and Gardens, Bristol, (401-253-2707)
Haffenreffer Museum of Anthropology, Bristol, (401-253-8388)
Herreshoff Marine and America's Cup Museum, Bristol (401-253-5000)
Mount Hope Farm, Bristol, (401-254-1745)

Accommodations:
Bradford Dimond Norris House, Bristol, (401-253-6338)
Bristol Harbor Inn, Bristol, (401-254-1444)
Point Pleasant Inn, Bristol, (401-253-0627)
Rockwell House Inn, Bristol, (401-253-0040)
William's Grant Inn, Bristol, (401-253-4222)

East Providence (Pomham Rocks Lighthouse)
Other Sites of Interest:
Crescent Park Looff Carousel, East Providence, (401-433-2828)
Governor Henry Lippitt House Museum, Providence, (401-453-0688)
Providence Athenaeum, Providence (401-421-6970)
Providence Children's Museum, Providence, (401-273-KIDS)
Roger Williams Park Zoo, Providence, (401-725-3510)

Accommodations:
AAA Jacob Hill Inn, Providence, (888-336-9165)
Johnson & Wales Inn, Providence (800-232-1772)
New Yorker Motor Lodge, East Providence, (401-434-8000)
State House Inn, Providence (401-351-6111)
The Cady House B & B, Providence (401-273-5398)

Jamestown (Conanicut North Light/ Beavertail Lighthouse/ Dutch Island Lighthouse)
Other Sites of Interest:
Fort Wetherill State Park, Jamestown, (401-222-2632)
Jamestown Museum, Jamestown, (401-423-0784)
Jamestown Windmill, Jamestown, (401-423-1798)

Newport Butterfly Farm, Middletown, (401-849-9519)
Newport Vineyards and Winery, Middletown, (401-848-5161)

Accommodations:
Adele Turner Inn, Newport, (401-847-1811)
Bay Voyage, Jamestown, (401-423-2100)
Howard Johnson Inn, Middletown, (401-849-2000)
Hydrangea House Inn, Newport, (401-846-4435)
Meadowlark Recreational Vehicle Park, Newport, (401-846-9455)

Little Compton (Sakonnet Point Lighthouse)
Other Sites of Interest:
Historic Fort Adams, Newport, (401-841-0707)
Little Compton Historical Society, Little Compton, (401-635-4035)
Newport Art Museum, Newport, (401-848-8200)
The Astors' Beechwood Mansion, Newport, (401-846-3772)
Wilbor House, Barn, and Quaker Meeting House, Little Compton, (401-635-4035)

Accommodations:
Chase Farm B&B, Newport, (401-845-9338)
Hotel Viking, Newport, (401-847-3300)
Newport Marriott, Newport, (401-849-1000)
Spring Street Inn, Newport, (401-847-4767)
Travelodge, Newport, (401-849-4700

Newport (Castle Hill Lighthouse/ Newport Harbor Light/ Rose Island Lighthouse)
Other Sites of Interest:
America's Cup Charters, Newport, (401-846-9886)
International Tennis Hall of Fame, Newport, (401-849-3990)
Museum of Newport History at the Brick Market, Newport, (401-841-8770)
New England Aquarium, Newport, (401-849-8490)
Newport Mansion Tours, Newport, (401-847-1000)

Accommodations:
Baldwin Place, Newport, (401-847-3801)
The Burbank Rose, Newport, (401-849-9457)
Cliffside Inn, Newport, (401-847-1811)
Newport Dinner Train, Newport, (401-841-8700)
Paradise Motel, Middletown, (401-847-1500)

North Kingstown (Plum Beach Light) / Wickford (Poplar Point Light)
Other Sites of Interest:
Casey Farm, North Kingstown, (401-295-1030)
Gilbert Stuart Birthplace, North Kingstown, (401-294-3001)
Quonset Aviation Museum, North Kingstown, (401-294-9540)
Smith's Castle, Wickford, (401-294-3521)
Wickford Village, Wickford, (401-294-4867)

Accommodations:
Boat House B&B, North Kingstown, (401-295-5010)
Budget Inn of North Kingstown, (401-294-4888)
Crosswinds Farm B&B, North Kingstown, (401-294-6168)
Haddie Pierce House, North Kingstown, (401-294-7674)
Welcome Inn, North Kingstown, (401-884-9153)

**Portsmouth (Hog Island Shoal Light)/
Prudence Island (Sandy Point Lighthouse)**
Other Sites of Interest:
Green Animals, Portsmouth, (401-847-1000)
Greenvale Vineyards, Portsmouth, (401-847-3777)
Narragansett Bay National Estuarine Sanctuary, Prudence Island, (401-683-6780)
Old School House, Portsmouth, (401-683-9178)

Accommodations:
Best Western Bay Point Inn & Conference Center, Portsmouth, 401-683-360
Founder's Brook Motel and Suites, Portsmouth, (401-683-1244)
Gardenview B&B, Newport, (401-849-5799)
Melville Ponds Campground, Portsmouth, (401-849-8212)
The Francis Malbone House, Newport, (401-846-0392)

Wakefield (Gooseberry Island Light/ Point Judith Lighthouse)
Other Sites of Interest:
Adventureland, Narragansett, (401-789-0030)
Fine Arts center Galleries, South Kingstown, (401-874-2775)
Hannah Robinson Rock and Tower, South Kingstown, (401-222-2632)
Historic Fayerweather House, South Kingstown, (401-789-9072)
South County Museum, Narragansett, (401-783-5400)

Accommodations:
Applewood Greene B&B, South Kingstown, (401-789-1937)
Blueberry Cove Inn, Narragansett, (401-792-9865)
Grinnell Inn, Narragansett, (401-789-4340)
Holiday Inn, South Kingstown, (401-789-1051)
Kagels Cottages, Narragansett, (401-783-4551)

Warwick (Conimicut Point Light/ Warwick Light)
Other Sites of Interest:
Goddard State Park, Warwick, (401-884-2010)
John Waterman Arnold House, Warwick, (401-467-7647)
Pawtuxet Village, Warwick , (401-738-2000)
Step Stone Falls, West Greenwich, (401-222-1157)
Warwick Museum of Art, Warwick, (401-737-0010)

Accommodations:
Comfort Inn Airport, Warwick, (401-732-0470)
Crowne Plaza Hotel at the Crossing, Warwick, (401-732-6000)
The Equinox Sailing Vessel, Warwick, (401-885-1822: summer; 941-263-6099: winter)

Henry L. Johnson House B&B, Warwick, (401-781-5158)
Radisson Airport Hotel, Warwick (401-739-3000)

Westerly (Watch Hill Lighthouse)
Other Sites of Interest:
Babcock-Smith House, Westerly, (401-596-5704)
Duck Land/Water Tours, Westerly, (401-596-7761)
Flying Horse Carousel, Westerly, (401-348-6540)
Frosty Drew Observatory, Charlestown, (401-364-9508)
Narragansett Indian Meeting House/Church (401-364-1100)

Accommodations:
Andrea Resort Hotel, Westerly, (401-348-8788)
Atlantic Beach Casino Resort, Westerly, (401-322-7100)
Harbour House Inn, Westerly, (401-596-7500)
Sand Castle Inn, Westerly, (401-596-6900)
Sandy Shore Motel and Apartments, Westerly, (401-596-5616)

Bibliography

Cassinelli, Ron, "Man of Stone," *Providence Journal*, January 14, 2000.

Marcus, Jon. *Lighthouses of New England: Your Guide to the Lighthouses of Maine, New Hampshire, Vermont, Massachusetts, Rhode Island, and Connecticut.* Stillwater, Minnesota: Voyageur Press, 2001.

Scott, Judi, "Lighthouse replica to be lifted into place," *South County* (Rhode Island) *Independent*, December 30, 1999, Volume 3.

Snow, Edward Rowe. *The Lighthouses of New England, 1716–1973.* New York: Dodd, Mead, 1973.

United States Coast Guard. *Light List. Volume I, Atlantic Coast from St. Croix River, Maine, to Toms River, New Jersey, First Coast Guard District.* Washington D.C.: Government Printing Office, 1999.

Works Progress Administration. *Connecticut: A Guide to Its Roads, Lore, and People.* American Guide Series. Boston: Houghton Mifflin Company, 1937.

Works Progress Administration. *Rhode Island, a Guide to the Smallest State.* American Guide Series. Boston: Houghton Mifflin Company, 1937.

General Lighthouse Websites:
Lighthouse Depot: www.lhdepot.com
National Park Service Maritime Heritage Program Inventory of Historic Light Stations: www.cr.nps.gov/maritime/ltaccess.html
New England Lighthouses: A Virtual Guide: www.lighthouse.cc/
United States Coast Guard Connecticut Light Stations: www.uscg.mil/hq/gcp/history/WEBLIGHTHOUSES/LHCT.html

Lighthouse-Specific Websites:
Avery Point Lighthouse Society: www.apls.tripod.com
Beavertail Lighthouse History: www.riparks.com/beavertailhistory.htm
Block Island North Light Fund: www.ctol.net/~rdaines/nlfund.html
Five Mile Point Lighthouse: www.newhavenparks.org/lighthouse_point.htm
Rose Island Lighthouse: www.roseislandlighthouse.org
Sheffield Island Lighthouse: www.seaport.org

All directions to the lighthouse are taken from www.lhdepot.com and are used with permission from the author. Special thanks to the American Lighthouse Foundation's Tim Harrison and Jeremy D'Entremont for their permission to use this and other information from the site.

Index

Aggasiz, Alexander	55
Avery Point Lighthouse	6–7
Beavertail Lighthouse	50–51
Black Rock Harbor Light	10-11
Brant Point Light	22-23
Bridgeport Breakwater Light	46-47
Bridgeport Harbor Light	47
Bristol Ferry Light	52-53
Brooks, Captain Oliver	9
Castle Hill Lighthouse	54-55
Chatham Rocks Light	38-39
Conanicut North Light	56-57
Conimicut Point Light	58-59, 67
Dutch Island Lighthouse	60-61
Fall River Steamboat Company	53
Faulkners Island Light	8–9, 19
Fayerweather Island Light	10-11
Five Mile Point Lighthouse	12-13
Gallup, Jay and David	63
Goat Island Light	68-69
Gooseberry Island Light	62-63
Great Captain Island Lighthouse	14-15
Greens Ledge Light	16-17, 29, 35
Gustavus, George	85
Hamilton R. Douglas Company	27
Hog Island Shoal Light	64-65
Hooper, John and Kimberly	63
Jefferson, Thomas	9, 91
Jordan, Frederick	31
Lynde Point Light	18-19
Melville, David	51
Middleground Light	44-45
Morgan Point Lighthouse	20–21
Mystic Seaport Lighthouse	22-23
Nayatt Point Lighthouse	9, 66-67
New Haven Breakwater Light	36-37
New Haven Harbor Light	12-13, 37
New London Harbor Lighthouse	9, 24-25
New London Ledge Lighthouse	19, 26 27
Newport Harbor Light	68-69
North Light	70-71, 86
Peck Ledge Light	28-29
Penfield Reef Light	30-31
Plum Beach Light	72-73
Point Judith Lighthouse	74-75
Pomham Rocks Lighthouse	76-77
Poplar Point Light	78-79
Prudence Island Lighthouse	84-85
Race Rock Light	31
Richardson, H.H.	55
Rose Island Lighthouse	80-81
Sakonnet Point Lighthouse	82-83
Sandy Point Light	70
Sandy Point Lighthouse	84-85
Saybrook Breakwater Lighthouse	32-33
Sheffield Island Light	34-35
Ship John Shoal Light	37
Smith, F. Hopkinson	31
Southeast Light	86-87
Southwest Ledge Light	36-37
Stamford Harbor Light	38-39, 59
Stonington Breakwater Light	41
Stonington Harbor Lighthouse	40-41
Stratford Point Lighthouse	42-43
Stratford Shoal Light	44-45
Tongue Point Light	46-47
Tynan, T.H.	86
Warwick Light	88-89
Washington, George	51
Watch Hill Lighthouse	90-91
Wickford Harbor Light	79
Woodward, Abisha	9

Notes

Notes

Notes

Notes

Notes

Notes